THE RIGHT WAY
TO
KEEP PIGEONS

Sean Mc Evoy

THE RIGHT WAY TO
KEEP PIGEONS

by

DAVID ROBINSON

PAPERFRONTS

ELLIOT RIGHT WAY BOOKS
KINGSWOOD, SURREY, U.K.

Made and Printed in Great Britain by Cox & Wyman Ltd.,
Reading.

CONTENTS

LIST OF ILLUSTRATIONS

1
The Pigeon

Everybody is familiar with the pigeon. It is a bird that frequents countryside and big city alike.

The pigeon belongs to the family 'Columbidae' of which there are some forty-nine species. The common pigeon is a direct descendant of the Rock Dove 'Columbidae Livia' which is the bird that was first domesticated many hundreds of years ago.

Through selective breeding the normal blue colour of the pigeon has been changed to those of red, white, black and many other variations of these colours. The homing sense has been developed to such an extent that the modern-day racing pigeon can negotiate a course of over five hundred miles in one day at very fast speeds.

The fancy pigeon has been developed into many strange forms in which the physical shape of the bird has been altered drastically. The Fantail, for instance, has a large peacock-style tail which almost covers the bird as it displays. The Fairy Swallow has long flowing feathers down its legs and feet; the Nun has a cowl of feathers covering the nape of the neck and the back of the head.

The pigeon is a bird that prefers to nest in holes and nooks where it is semi-dark and secluded. The nest site is either a cliff face or a ledge on a building. It is sparsely furnished with a few sticks and feathers, more of a token than a nest proper. Although the nesting material is scanty, each piece is brought separately by the male. The loving and caring nature of the pigeon pair is a sight to be marvelled at. They are very attentive to each other and the cock bird can become very jealous of a male rival should he trespass too near the female or their nest. In the Racing Pigeon, the jealousy of the cock bird is exploited to try and make the bird fly home faster. In practice this works very well and some fantastic performances have been recorded using this system which is referred to as the 'Widowhood' method.

The female pigeon or hen lays two white eggs approximately ten days after mating. Both sexes incubate the eggs but the hen will sit on them for most of the time; the cock will perform his share of the incubation from about ten o'clock in the morning until about an hour before nightfall. The young pigeons or squabs are hatched after an incubation period of about eighteen days from the laying of the second egg. Both eggs usually hatch together on the morning of the eighteenth day.

The youngsters are born with a fine yellow down which covers all the body although it is sparse when compared with that of the chicken. The young pigeon is blind at birth, its eyes opening after about four days. From birth to five days old the parents feed their youngsters on a milk that is formed in the crop. From five days onward the youngsters receive seeds and corn that are soaked in water whilst lying in the parent bird's crop. The growth rate of the young pigeon is rapid and by the twenty-eighth day the babies can feed themselves and are almost fully feathered except for underneath the wing.

The pigeon has a defined breeding season from early January until late September.

It is thought that pigeons were first domesticated as a source of food during the Middle Ages. In fact there are many Dovecots still standing today that were built around this time. Certainly the pigeons were given their freedom during the day and spent most of their time foraging in the fields and farmyards.

Pigeons are still a delicacy to this day and in many eastern countries they are bred specially for the hotel trade and the gourmet's table. Pigeons are kept as pets the world over; their plumage colours and types are many and varied which makes them so attractive. Their antics are very endearing and they can become very tame indeed. The pigeon's voice can be very soothing as it consists of a very soft 'coo-coo' call. The cock pigeon has a very distinctive and attractive mating display.

The cock actually courts the hen and spins round and round in display cooing all the time and dragging his tail along the floor as he rushes towards the hen.

The pigeon is a master of the air and is built with speed in mind. The flight feathers of the wing are long and when folded against the bird's body meet at a point about an inch from the end of the tail. The tail itself is narrow and when fanned out provides the pigeon with a very efficient air brake. The normal wild colour of the pigeon is slate blue with a greenish-purple neck and black double wing bars. The neck coloration is very attractive because it can be described as iridescent. The neck feathers shine with an almost metallic look. This type of pattern is known as blue-barred, and pigeon fanciers refer to it as, simply, blue. A slight variation of the blue-barred pattern is that of chequered. The slate blue base colour is still present but in the chequer the wing bars are broken into a type of dappled pattern which extends all over the pigeon's wing and shoulder. The chequered pattern can be seen as very light or very dark in which latter case the colour is almost completely self black.

The pigeon's staple diet consists of both large and small seeds, greenfood such as young tender leaves and shoots, and perhaps the odd grub or insect. Certainly domestic pigeons are known to take slugs and snails from the garden.

The pigeon's food is stored in the bird's crop where it is mixed with water and softened. The softened food is then ground into a pulp with the help of grit. The grit consists of particles of stone and earth which are deliberately swallowed by the pigeon in order to assist with the digestion process.

Feral pigeons will congregate around corn mills in order to glean whatever corn is spilled over the ground, they will also be found wherever there is food or food scraps. Well-known examples of this are the hundreds of feral pigeons that can be seen in Trafalgar Square in London. These pigeons are extremely well fed by countless tourists every day of the year. Pigeons are creatures of habit and will congregate at a certain spot at the same time every day if they learn that food will be available at that precise moment.

The Skeleton

The bones which form the skeleton have two main functions: they are a framework which adds rigidity to the body and helps the pigeon to stand; the skeleton also helps protect the vital organs of the body. For instance the heart, lungs, and liver are all encased within the rib cage and the brain within the skull.

The texture and composition of the bones differs according to where each bone is located, and the purpose of the bone. For instance the skull is made from bone that is quite hard and will withstand some very hard knocks. The rib cage bones, or the ribs, are made from bone that is much softer than the skull. These ribs have joints that are very elastic because they have to move as the body contorts itself whilst going through everyday functions. There are bones which carry blood vessels and marrow to feed and nourish other parts of the body.

The bone structure of the pigeon is particularly interesting in that many of the bones are very light in weight. These include the bones of the wing and shoulder regions. Lightness is very important in the pigeon's wing because the powers of flight have to be unhindered. If these bones are looked at through a cross-section it will be seen that they are full of air sacs which make them very light and buoyant.

The pigeon's skull is typical of most birds in that it is very light and yet very strong. A very interesting fact is that the upper beak or mandible can be moved independently of the upper jaw. In mammals the top half of the jaw is fixed and rigid and therefore cannot be moved. The pigeon has a type of lever which acts on the beak by way of a strip of soft flexible bone that is situated just below the upper jaw. Another interesting point is that the lower jaw of the pigeon can be completely detached from the upper jaw. This characteristic is very typical of the bird family because many

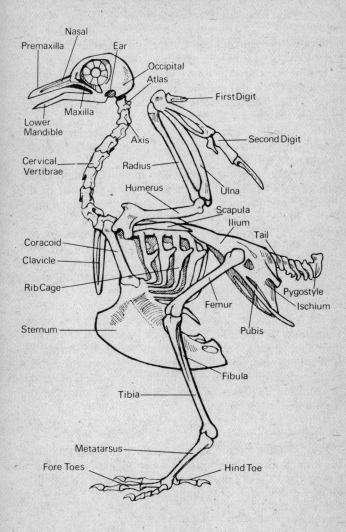

Fig. 1 The skeleton of the pigeon

of them have to swallow their food whole. e.g. Birds of Prey and seabirds.

Because the pigeon has quite large eyes in relation to the size of the head it also has large eye sockets in the skull.

The neck or Cervical vertebrae consist of small bones which interlock and provide the neck with its manoeuvrability. The Cervical vertebrae extend right down the pigeon's back and so form the spine.

The shoulder blade is attached to the collar bone at the base of the neck and so forms the wishbone as it is better known.

The pigeon's rib cage is fused to the backbone to give it strength; the ends of the ribs are in turn attached to the breastbone or sternum. This bone is in fact the most vital of all the bones which protect the organs of the body. The breast bone, or keel as it is referred to by pigeon fanciers, has to withstand some very severe shocks, such as when the bird strikes an object whilst in flight.

The pelvic girdle of the pigeon is near the centre of gravity allowing the bird to stand without relying on its tail to steady it. The leg is in fact made up of three main bones, the femur or thigh bone, the tibia or shin bone, and the metatarsus which is in fact the foot. If the reader compares the human leg bones to that of the pigeon as shown in Fig. 1 it will be seen that the pigeon actually stands on tip-toe for the whole of the time. If a human was to crouch for the whole of his life, he would in fact take up the stance normally taken by the pigeon and other birds.

The Internal Anatomy

Pigeons have internal organs that are grouped very close together within the body. This compact arrangement ensures that the organs take up as little room as possible to allow for the extra large flight muscles.

The Heart

The heart pumps the blood around the body. The blood enters the heart on one side; it enters the chamber of the

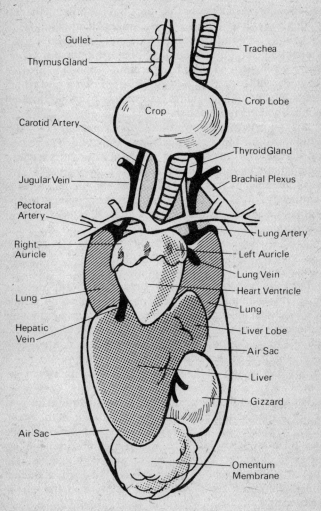

Gullet

Thymus Gland

Trachea

Crop Lobe

Crop

Carotid Artery

Thyroid Gland

Jugular Vein

Brachial Plexus

Pectoral Artery

Lung Artery

Right Auricle

Left Auricle

Lung Vein

Lung

Heart Ventricle

Lung

Hepatic Vein

Liver Lobe

Air Sac

Liver

Gizzard

Air Sac

Omentum Membrane

Fig. 2 The internal organs

heart and is pumped across into the other chamber by way of a contracting action. The blood is then divided into two vessels, one which leads to the lungs and the other to the rest of the body. The blood which is pumped into the lungs releases its cargo of carbon dioxide and takes in oxygen.

From the lungs the blood travels back into the heart from where it is in turn pumped back around the body to provide the body with sustenance. It is estimated that a bird which weighs one pound can pump four ounces of blood through its heart every sixty seconds.

It is not generally known that birds have a pair of jugular veins whilst all other mammals have only one. The reason for this is the fact that the bird has the ability to turn its head right round to face backwards (180°). Whenever a bird turns its head in this manner one of the jugular veins is completely cut off but the blood that is being pumped to the brain is automatically transferred to the other jugular where it continues its journey.

The Liver

The liver is one of the largest organs within the pigeon's body. It has a number of functions. Firstly it produces bile which acts on the digestion by breaking up food matter into proteins and other substances.

The liver also produces urea from the process of breaking down the protein by way of chemical changes. Urea is a waste product and is secreted from the body by way of the urine.

The liver also has the ability to convert sugar into energy, or it can convert the sugar into fat and store it in the body. When large amounts of energy are required by the body the liver releases glycogen into the blood stream. Adrenalin has a stimulating effect on the liver causing it to release large amounts of glycogen in order to give the body a sudden boost such as in times of excitement or when the bird is frightened.

The Kidneys

The pigeon's kidneys are the organs which collect waste products from the blood stream. These substances consist of excess sugar, carbonates, nitrogen and poisons.

The kidneys are protected by the pelvic girdle and can be found at the back of the body near the spine.

The pigeon does not pass urine in the same manner as mammals because it cannot pass liquids. Instead the urine is mixed with the faeces and can be seen as the white part of this matter.

The Intestines

These organs constitute the contents of the abdomen such as the Pancreas, the duodenum, caecum, and the cloaca.

Food is passed along the intestines from the gullet; as it passes through the stomach it is acted upon by chemical substances such as bile which break up the solid matter into liquid. From the liquid all the proteins and blood sugars are extracted and distributed throughout the body via the blood.

The Crop

The pigeon's crop is situated just over the front of the breast at the base of the gullet. Food is passed down the gullet where it is mixed with saliva from the mouth and passes into the crop.

Water is taken in by the pigeon when it drinks, and softens the hard shells of the corn and seeds that it eats. The mush of food is then passed into the gizzard where it is further broken up by the grit that the pigeon swallows. Pigeon grit that is fed to domestic birds consists mainly of limestone flints or crushed sea shells. It can be seen that the organ which contains these sharp pieces of stone etc. has to be very tough indeed. The crop of a pigeon also produces a substance known as pigeon milk. This is produced by the crop by an action concerned with the birds hormones. The inner lining of the crop thickens greatly as the hatching of the eggs nears. The cells produced by this thickening of the crop walls fall off and are turned into a curd known as the pigeon's milk.

The pigeon does not produce a true milk as is seen in mammals, it is merely a mixture of protein and fat which contains no sugar at all. This remarkable action is done by both sexes, a characteristic which is not repeated in any other branch of the bird family.

The Tongue

It may seem a little strange including the pigeon's tongue in a description of the pigeon's anatomy. However, the bird's tongue is very interesting indeed. For instance it was often supposed that because the pigeon merely swallows its food whole it has no sense of taste; this is now known not to be so. A pigeon that has never eaten certain seeds will often pick these out from a mixture containing these and other varieties of seed.

If substances are added to the pigeon's drinking water that taste strongly it will be found that once the pigeon has tasted the water it will not drink from it again.

Pigeons will prefer to eat smooth-sided seeds rather than those with wrinkled sides such as the pea.

The Feathers

The pigeon's feathers are in fact hairs that are adapted to a different environment from that of other creatures, which do not fly and so require a different covering to their body.

Feathers appear from under the skin in the same way as do hairs; they are controlled by muscles which can determine as to what angle the feather lies. When it is cold the feathers are fluffed out to trap warm air and so insulate the bird. Mammals cause their hair to stand in the same manner whenever they are cold.

There are many different types of feather on a pigeon's body as will be seen in Fig. 3. There are feathers which provide the bird with the power of flight, feathers which are very small and light to provide both insulation and protection. The larger feathers of the pigeon's body are known as contour feathers and number the flights and tail feathers amongst their group. These feathers are made up of a central quill and the vane, which is in fact a simple hair that has barbs or hooks along its entire length. These barbs act in the same way as a zipper we use on our clothes. Whenever the barbs are pulled apart the pigeon merely strokes its beak along the vane and the barbs come together again.

The small body feathers do not have these barbs as they are soft and downy in texture. The feathers are kept in good condition by the act of preening and regular baths. Pigeons love to bathe, especially youngsters.

Young pigeons do everything just by nature, they are not taught to preen themselves and yet they can be seen busily

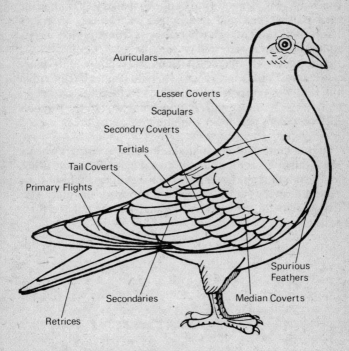

Fig. 3 The pigeon's feathers

preening away whilst nestlings and still unable to feed themselves. Young pigeons take to water almost as readily as ducklings, they will splash about in their bath showing no fear of the water at all.

At the base of the tail there is a gland which extrudes oil. The pigeon merely pinches the gland with its bill and smears the oil over its beak. The oil is then transferred to the feathers during preening.

Pigeons that are not handled regularly take on a bloom all over their feathers. This bloom is a good indication that all is well with the pigeon as it means that the plumage is in good condition, and if the plumage is in good condition the bird's health must also be right. A sick bird will neglect its preening. Another good indication that all is well is when the bird shakes itself and re-arranges its feathers, when this happens a cloud of dust will often rise from the bird. This is in fact the bloom referred to earlier.

The pigeon's feathers also tell us other things, for instance when a fret mark appears across a flight feather it tells us that the bird was under stress when this feather was growing.

The moult is a very, very important part of the pigeon's life. In racing pigeons it can either make or break a good racing bird.

It is so important that many racing pigeon fanciers will not let out their birds for exercise when the end flight is growing.

The moult is a process whereby the feathers of the bird are renewed every year. They are dropped in succession beginning with the head and ending with the tail and flight feathers.

2

Pigeon Lofts and Dovecots

Perhaps the most essential piece of equipment the prospective pigeon fancier needs is the pigeon loft where the birds will be housed.

There are some basic rules and regulations that should be followed if the loft is to be practical and useful for the purpose. For the comfort of the birds it should be completely dry; it should be quite draught proof, and yet it should be as well ventilated as possible.

For the purposes of the pigeon fancier it should be easily accessible at all times and in all weathers. The loft interior should be designed so as to allow the everyday management tasks to be carried out efficiently without any complications.

For the sake of the neighbours the loft should blend in with the local environment; it should be of a neat design that looks tidy and clean at all times. Nothing gives the name of pigeon-keeping more of a bad image than a dirty, untidy eyesore of a loft.

Food of any description should be stored well away from the loft if possible or failing this it should be kept in vermin-proof containers where mice and rats will not be attracted to it.

Siting the Loft

Without doubt the best site for your loft is where it will be as high as possible without being obtrusive. Common sense should tell us that if we were to place our loft at the bottom of a hill or in a hollow we will soon be flooded out should stormy weather occur.

Most gardens are quite level and so we should endeavour to lift the loft as high as possible from the ground. A height of around 60 centimetres should be the minimum to allow for good air circulation, and also to keep the underside of the floor free from damp.

Brick pillars are ideal for this purpose and they can be built quite easily and cheaply. As an alternative wooden railway sleepers can be utilised. This type of timber can often be purchased quite cheaply from any scrap timber yard. The railway sleeper is especially useful as it is impregnated with tar to protect it.

The siting of the loft can also be determined by local Council rules. In some areas the keeping of pigeons on Council property is not allowed and usually Councils will make provision for the hobby on a nearby pen or allotment. If a loft can be erected with the Council's permission it usually has to be a given distance away from the house itself.

A person with a quite long garden should site the loft as far from houses as possible because pigeons should never be allowed to roost on the house tops, especially those of neighbours.

After exercise the birds should be made to land on the loft itself and not make a nuisance of themselves on other people's property.

Ideally the loft should face south, as this will allow the greatest amount of sunshine to warm the loft for most of the day. West winds are usually wet winds, east and north winds are usually cold winds and they should all be prevented from blowing directly onto the loft front if at all possible.

Loft Size

The loft size will depend firstly, on the amount of room that is available in which to site the loft; secondly the availability of a suitable type of building that can be converted into a good pigeon loft. This usually entails the conversion of the family garden shed, perhaps much to the disgust of the rest of the members of the family. Thirdly, if a suitable building is not available, the depth of one's pocket. Pigeon lofts can be bought that are of a standard size and can be ordered from any of the reputable loft-making firms that are advertised in the pigeon fancy press. These firms will also make pigeon lofts to your special instructions if required.

The pigeon loft should be of a size appropriate to that of the fancier. In other words it is little use having a loft that is too small for your comfort. There is nothing worse than having to squeeze through narrow doorways or crouch low once inside the loft. Such conditions make the fancier unhappy, and if the fancier is unhappy then it stands to reason that his birds will be unhappy too.

Exterior Design

Loft designs have taken great steps forward in recent years, notably with the inception of the louvred door. At one time every pigeon loft had a dowelled front. Today this is not always the case, because many lofts incorporate the closed-in front with either adjustable or fixed louvres installed. In the case of the closed-in front the movement of fresh air is made possible with the louvred panels and light is let into the loft through glass or perspex panels that are let into the roof.

The racing pigeon lofts of today do not have a trap whereby the birds enter the loft. Instead they use the open door method which entails the opening of either sliding or hinged doors on the front of the loft. After the pigeon has entered the loft the doors are merely closed behind it. A further sophistication of this method is the trapping corridor, which is simply an empty compartment which the bird enters before it enters the loft proper. During racing the rubber ring can be taken from the pigeon without fear of its escaping capture.

Perhaps the most important aspect of the loft is the roof, for if it leaks during rain it will cause damp patches within the loft, aiding the spread of disease. Ideally the loft should have a roof that is covered with roofing felt or is made of corrugated asbestos. The roof should overhang at the back and the front by at least 15 centimetres so that rain will not run down the walls.

There is some argument as to whether the roof should slope to the front or the back of the loft. If the roof slopes to the front the rain will drip onto the fancier if he should have

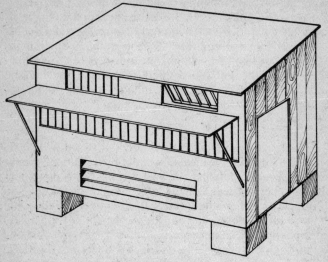

Fig. 4 A typical pigeon loft

to stand there either whilst opening a door or other task. The advantage with a roof that slopes to the front is that any birds that land on the loft roof can be easily seen. However any bird that does land there is in the wrong place anyway, as it should either land on the landing board or go through the open doors.

If the roof slopes to the back the rain will not interfere with the fancier in any way, but any bird that lands there cannot be seen from the front of the loft.

Most conventional pigeon lofts have a front that is half dowelled or made from stout laths. This is to facilitate the easy entry of fresh air and light. About two thirds of the way up the front there is usually a landing board onto which the pigeons should pitch after their exercise. The landing board should not be too narrow, a width of about 60 to 80 centimetres is quite adequate.

The birds will enter the loft through a small trap door at the top of the loft or through bob wires which are hung there. The bob wires are now considered old-fashioned, but nevertheless they still do a great job. Basically the idea of bob wires is to allow the pigeon easy entry through them and also prevent the bird from getting back out again.

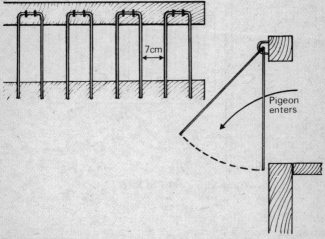

Fig. 5 Bob wires

Some pigeon lofts have a trap installed on their front, which is a type of cage as shown in Fig. 6. There is no real advantage in this kind of equipment except that it gives youngsters and new birds the opportunity of seeing the outside world from within the loft.

There are no hard and fast rules about where the human's entrance door should be. Normally it is situated at the side of the building but there is no reason why it should not be installed at the front.

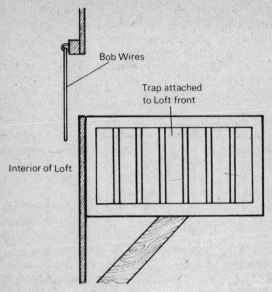

Fig. 6   Trap attached to front of loft

Pigeons soon get used to the sight of their owner entering and leaving through the door. Sliding doors are without doubt the best type to instal, although they can be expensive. Hinged doors should open inwards to help prevent the escape of any birds that are not allowed their freedom, such as valuable stock birds. It is harder for a bird to fly over the fanciers shoulder if the door opens inwards because there is less space for the bird to get through.

The addition of louvres as mentioned earlier is now considered to be very important in modern pigeon loft design. The louvres provide a constant and steady flow of air into the loft and are best situated as low down as possible. Warm air rises and the fouled air should be able to escape from the loft through ventilation holes that are drilled along the top of the rear wall. The fancier's nose should tell him whether there is enough good ventilation in his loft.

Interior design

The interior of the pigeon loft is important as regards ease of movement and comfort. The average pigeon fancier will spend a great amount of time inside his loft and so it has to be designed so that he can move about with ease without frightening his birds.

Maximum consideration must be given to the best method of ensuring that there is no space wasted. Every nook and cranny should be used to its full advantage.

By the same rule this does not mean that there should be any overcrowding of the inmates.

Many modern-day pigeon lofts have a trapping corridor in them which helps to ensure that birds returning from a race can be caught up quite easily before they enter their respective compartments. The corridor also gives the fancier room to move about without disturbing his birds too much. Most lofts are divided into two compartments, one for young birds, and one for old birds. If the loft is of a size that

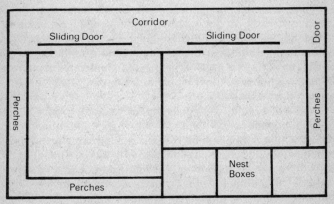

Fig. 7 Typical loft plan. This loft is the right size for about 24 pigeons.

can be divided further then it is advantageous to do this. Further compartments can be used for stock birds or as a corn and basket store. If fancy pigeons are kept, the extra compartment will serve as a penning room where the birds can be trained to stand in the show pen.

The usual size of a compartment will be about two metres square, but the exact shape does not matter provided there is room for the fancier to move about in comfort. Entrance to these compartments can be gained either through the loft door from the outside, or from the corridor if one is included. Again it is better to use sliding doors as they are easier to open and do not require so much space to operate.

A height of 3.25 metres at the front of the loft is high enough for anyone and perhaps 2 metres at the back. If the roof is any higher than this it means that the birds will have space to fly over the fancier's head and they will be that much harder to handle and tame; also escapes of valuable stock birds can occur.

Perches

Perches are perhaps the most important pieces of loft furniture that the fancier has to provide.

There are two main types of perch. Firstly, there is the box perch which is probably the derivation of the expression 'pigeon hole'. As can be seen from the diagram the box perch is made from flat boards that interlock to provide the bird with an individual perch. The pigeon is protected from its neighbour directly above it and it is also segregated from its neighbours on either side.

To be of benefit to the pigeon, the box perch should be at least 15 centimetres wide and measure 30 x 30 centimetres. Perches that are made smaller than this tend to make the bird uncomfortable because it can be soiled by the bird above and also its other neighbours can reach it and peck at it. The novice will find that the bigger the box perches, the less they will be soiled by the birds, as the droppings will all be deposited on the loft floor.

The second type of perch is that of the inverted 'Vee',

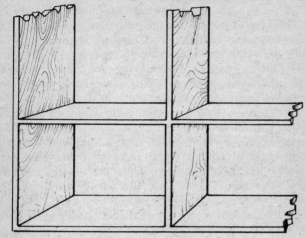

Fig. 8 Box perches

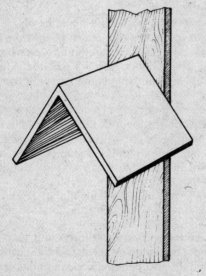

Fig. 9 A 'V' perch

which is as the name suggests merely two pieces of timber fastened together making a central ridge for the bird to stand on. This type of perch is very popular amongst the Belgian fanciers and also amongst fancy pigeon enthusiasts.

The vee perch can be fastened to the loft wall wherever there is sufficient space. The perching bird cannot be soiled by its upstairs neighbour because the winged section of the perch above protects him like an umbrella. If the Vee perches are sufficiently spaced apart there is no danger of the birds pecking each other and damaging each other's plumage.

Pigeons are very quarrelsome creatures especially when it comes to their territorial rights and some birds will take it into their heads that they own all the perches in a row and will fiercely defend them. This is very true of young cocks who are establishing their rights within the loft. There is definitely a pecking order within the loft, and the poor bird who is at the bottom of the order is in for a rough time although at times he will show remarkable courage in defending his little patch.

Perches of whatever type should never be placed where there are draughts or where rain is driven into the loft.

To prevent escapes, the perches should never be placed either beside or above doors. Perches that are difficult to clean are of no use at all and they should never be installed in the first place.

It should be the aim of every pigeon fancier to have more perches than he has birds; by following this golden rule the fancier will be assured that he will not be overcrowded. The only exception might apply in the young bird loft where a natural reduction in numbers usually takes place through replacement of lost birds in the racing loft.

Nest Boxes

Nest boxes are the second most important item of loft furniture. In size they should be at least 60 x 45 centimetres. The nest box should also be easy to clean and therefore it should have a front that can be taken away completely. In

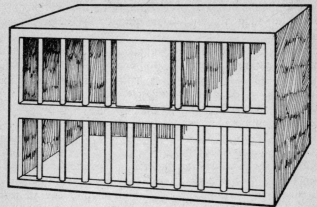

Fig. 10 Nest box. When opened, the door comes down like a drawbridge and lies flat, providing a perch for the bird which is not sitting on the eggs.

this way the birds' droppings can be scraped up and brushed out quite easily.

Easy access to the inside of the nest box is very important for other reasons. For instance a periodical check should be made on newly hatched youngsters, or youngsters that have just been ringed to ensure that the rings are still in place. The sizes given above are a minimum size to ensure that the birds have sufficient room to breed without any difficulties.

When the pairs are first put together they have to be locked in their boxes to ensure that they are truly paired and if you want to ensure that the parentage of the forthcoming youngsters can be guaranteed. Pigeon hens sometimes have very loose morals and can be mated by other cocks quite easily should the cock be so inclined. One way to prevent this is for the pair to have room to mate within the nest box, and also there must be enough room for two nest bowls because when the youngsters of one nest reach the age of about twenty-one days the hen will want to lay again. If there is insufficient room the youngsters will be turfed out of their nest whilst the hen lays again. If the youngsters decide to go back into their nest they could quite easily break the new eggs.

Nest box fronts are made from a light wooden frame into which dowels are fitted. The nest box front should have an opening that will allow the easy entry of the pigeon. If the entrance is restricted in any way it would be very difficult for a bird that had entered the wrong nest box to escape without causing damage to either the eggs or youngsters.

Some kind of door and perch has to be fitted to the nest box opening to allow one of the pair of pigeons to perch outside the box whilst the other either sits the eggs or broods the young. The door is used to lock the pair in their box either to pair them up or to accustom them to their nesting site.

The widowhood nestbox (mentioned more fully on page 70) is different from the conventional type of nest box in that it is designed to keep the cock and the hen separated – these types of nest box fronts are sometimes known as widowhood gates and are usually made from plastic.

Both the ordinary nest box front and the widowhood type of nest box front can be bought quite cheaply making it impractical for them to be made at home.

The nest boxes themselves can either be made at home or they too can be bought from pigeon equipment suppliers. Nest boxes can either be made or bought as a single box or as a unit of two or three and multiples of these. To keep fighting to a minimum it is better not to use perches as described on page 28 in the breeding compartment of the loft.

Instead the perch and door combined should be used so that the only place a cock can perch is on his own nest box front.

If he were to perch on any box but his own he would soon be chased away by the irate owner. Young cocks take great delight in trying to rule as many nest boxes as they possibly can. They are a nuisance within the loft and have to be managed with a firm hand.

Feeding Troughs

Feeding troughs and bowls can be purchased from pigeon equipment suppliers or they can be made quite easily at home.

Those that are bought are usually made from galvanised metal or plastic.

The most usual form of feeder trough for pigeons is a long narrow one that is covered over the top to prevent the birds from fouling it. Circular feeders can be obtained but these are not as popular as the troughs. Unless food is to be left before the pigeons at all times the troughs should be removed during the day to prevent them being soiled.

A wooden feeding trough can be made quite easily by nailing two pieces of wood together in the shape of a 'V' and attaching a block of wood at each end to act as feet. Alternatively a feeding vessel can be made by making a simple wooden tray with two centimetre high sides. These are shown in Fig. 11.

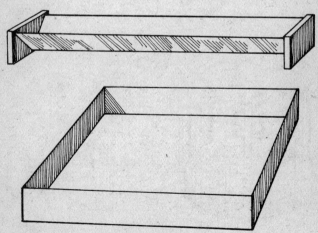

Fig. 11 Feeding trays or hoppers

After every feeding session the feeding troughs should be removed and scraped clean before being put away. There are a good many pigeon fanciers who do not use feeding vessels at all but prefer to feed straight onto the loft floor. This method is fine provided that the loft floor is kept clean at all times and any excess food is swept up straight away after feeding times. Leaving food to be soiled by the birds is inviting disease.

Water Fountains

Vessels for water are very, very important to the pigeon fancier. More diseases are spread by water than any other means of infection and so the water must be kept scrupulously clean at all times.

The most common type of water fountain as used for pigeons is the type that incorporates a round bowl surrounded by wire dowels and covered by a pointed top. The pointed top ensures that the birds cannot perch on the fountain and foul the water. The wire dowel surround

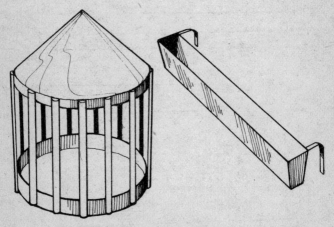

Fig. 12   A water fountain and a trough

ensures that the water is used for drinking and not for bathing and so it keeps the birds out of the water. These fountains can be bought in plastic, galvanised metal or enamel. The only drawback with this type of fountain is that it should be placed on a shelf that is well off the loft floor to prevent debris from blowing into it. Also the birds cannot drink all the water before the next water change and therefore any medication that may have been added to it will be wasted.

Watering troughs that can be hung on the outside of the compartment are much easier to use and much more hygienic. It is impossible for them to be fouled by the birds and they only hold sufficient water to last the birds until the next water change. These troughs are also very handy for training the young racing pigeon to drink from them whilst in the basket. When race birds are held over until the next day only those that have been schooled in this way will know where to find water. A racing pigeon that is thirsty will drop down whenever it sees water and so waste valuable time in doing so. This is when many racing pigeons are shot by so-called sportsmen. Drinking water for pigeons should be changed as often as the opportunity presents itself. Many fanciers change the water two or three times per day but there is really no need to go to such extreme lengths. Every time the water is changed the bowl should be swilled out, and at least once per week the whole fountain should be scrubbed out completely with hot water and a disinfectant.

Sterilizing agents can be added to the daily drinking water to help keep the risk of infection to a minimum.

In the same manner some fanciers add glucose and other tonics to the drinking water to try and gain the best possible advantage over their fellow-fanciers in competition.

Baths

All pigeons love to bathe, and will do so in all kinds of weather, whether it be roasting hot or a couple of inches deep in snow. Provision should therefore be made for the pigeons to have their weekly bath. Almost anything can be used and more often than not this is what happens. The most popular choice of a pigeon bath is one of the old Victorian stone kitchen sinks that is stood on four bricks. Any kind of vessel can be used provided it is clean and can be emptied easily. Bath water should never be allowed to stand for more than twenty-four hours before being tipped away.

Remember disease can be spread by water and we must always be on our guard.

The pigeon's bath should be placed where there is no danger of the birds being preyed upon by cats. This can be very difficult and many fanciers resort to placing the bath on the loft roof; even then wire netting should be placed all round the eaves to deter cats from leaping onto the roof. Bathtime in the loft usually means a time of relaxation and rest, when the birds can thoroughly enjoy themselves in the water and then lounge about the loft as they dry. The usual day for this enjoyable event is on a Sunday morning especially after a hard day's racing the day before.

Cleanliness and Sanitation

Cleanliness is essential in all aspects of pigeon keeping.

Cleaning out is a job that should be done every single day if possible and to this end there is nothing to beat the good old fashioned scraper and handbrush. The piles of droppings should be removed away from the loft site and not left in heaps for the flies to feed on.

Some fanciers prefer to remove the birds from the loft whilst cleaning out but it is certain that if the birds are present they soon become used to the clatter and become much steadier in the fancier's presence. After scraping out, the perches and floor can be dusted with a dressing such as sand, or lime. In fact there are commercial dressings which the fancier can buy that are also a disinfectant and kill any germs that may be present.

Other fanciers prefer to use the deep litter method which involves the use of either sand, wood shavings, or sawdust on the loft floor to a depth of about 15 centimetres. This litter is only removed once per year because at weekly intervals lime is added to it and the whole lot raked over. It is claimed that a bacterial build up kills all undesirable germs, keeping the loft clean with the minimum of effort.

Every week the loft tools, feeding and watering vessels should be washed in hot soapy water and dried thoroughly before being returned to the loft.

Dovecots

The Dovecot or 'Cote' as it is more often referred to, is not as common as it used to be. At one time nearly every country home had a dovecot situated in the grounds. This was purely for decoration purposes and the pigeons that were kept were pets and were at liberty to come and go as they pleased. The usual type of pigeon kept in a dovecot were cross-bred Fantails. These birds were usually crossed with Tumblers so that they would have some sort of homing sense. The pure-bred Fantail is lacking in this basic pigeon faculty to some extent and cannot be relied upon to return to the dovecot at night. The pure-bred Fantail would also have difficulty in flying because of its peacock-style tail.

The dovecot itself is merely a small house that is attached to the end of an upright post, or hung on a convenient wall. The more elaborate types have ornate mouldings on the exterior and would be perhaps two or three storeys high. The birds would gain access by means of the 'Pigeon hole', which is merely a six inch square hole cut into the side of the dovecot. There would in fact be a number of pigeon holes each facing a different direction e.g. North, South, East and West.

It is important that dovecots are completely weather proof and are kept in good repair. Such a home for pigeons would become deserted should it fall into a state of disrepair; the birds would merely forsake the dovecot and perch upon the house roof at night.

The dovecot that is hung on the wall need not be anything more elaborate than a suitable wooden box. The box must have some form of shelter and a strip of wood along the front for the birds to alight upon. The sheltered part of the dovecot will also serve as a nest box should the birds be inclined to breed. Dovecots should be positioned where they can be easily seen from the house and they should most certainly be out of reach of marauding cats. The pigeon keeper must also be able to gain easy access to the dovecot in order to feed and water the birds.

Pigeon droppings can become a nuisance in the vicinity of the dovecot but, if a constant vigil is kept and the mess cleared up as soon as it appears, then there should be no problem.

3

Foods and Feeding

Pigeons are primarily grain feeders but they are very adaptable in their eating habits and will consume almost anything within reason.

Besides the usual seeds and corn, pigeons will eat plant leaves, fruit buds, and many forms of insect life as well as snails and slugs.

The modern-day pigeon fancier is very lucky indeed in that he has at his disposal a vast range of products that will ensure the nourishment and well-being of his birds. At one time pigeons were fed the gleanings from the local corn mill and whatever small seeds and cereals could be bought. Absolute cleanliness was not considered to be very important. Today, only the very best will suffice and any corn mixture not of the best quality and cleanliness is useless to the discerning pigeon fancier.

The mixtures that are marketed today are highly polished and contain no dust or dirt whatsoever. There are grain mixtures for every conceivable purpose, i.e. moulting, rearing, racing, and even resting mixtures. The feeding values of these mixtures differ according to the protein and carbohydrate content. For instance, where muscle is needed, the mixture will need to have a superior amount of protein contained within it for the bird to be able to build up good strong wing muscles.

During the breeding season the fat or carbohydrate content will have to be high and so the contents of the mixture are graded accordingly. The most modern advance in the field of pigeon feeding is the pellet, which is a compound feed that contains all the vital vitamins and minerals in their correct proportions.

The smaller seeds also have their part to play in feeding

pigeons; the small seeds are usually very high in their oil content and therefore are highly prized for their use in conditioning the birds for the show pen. These seeds are also well liked by the birds and are served as a treat, or as a bait in getting the pigeon to come into the loft when called.

Grit

Because the pigeon has no teeth, grit has to be provided at all times so that the birds can digest their food properly. Here again there are quite a number of grits that can be used. The main grit used to feed pigeons is shellfish grit, which is in fact the crushed seashells that we find on the beaches around our coastline. These shells are ground to a suitable size and washed until they are perfectly clean. Pigeons will eat grit greedily when feeding large youngsters, especially shellfish grit which contains sea salts. Limestone grit is also very popular, as is crushed brick, which as the title suggests is just an ordinary household brick crushed to suitable sized fragments.

Common Pigeon Foods

Below are described some of the main types of grain used in modern pigeon food mixtures. The feeding values of each grain are given both in the content percentages and also in the amount of calories that they contain. These figures are provided as a guide to the fancier who wishes to make up his or her own mixtures according to the use that they are needed for.

The first grains described all belong to the Legume family which have the ability to extract nitrogen from the soil in which they grow and transfer it into protein within their seeds.

MAPLE PEAS

These are the most common type of pea used in pigeon corn mixtures. In colour they are mottled brown, and are either wrinkled or smooth. Beneath the tough outer shell the pea is golden yellow in colour with a white flesh. They taste very much like the ordinary garden pea with which we are so familiar, but they do have a slightly more bitter tang on the tongue. Maple peas are grown in Australia, New Zealand, Canada, and the British Isles. The feeding value of the Maple Pea is as follows, it contains fourteen per cent water (which is relatively high), twenty-two per cent protein, and sixty per cent carbohydrate. There is almost no fat in the pea and very little fibre at 4%.

One pound of Maple Peas would contain approximately 1,405 calories. Very similar to the Maple Pea is the Israeli Dun Pea or Cow Pea. This grain has exactly the same feeding values as the Maple Pea except that it has a calorie content of 1,430 per pound which is slightly higher.

TIC BEANS

This is a bean that can either be used in a mixture or it can be fed on its own with no additives. The bean is large compared to the pea and has a black or dark brown eye at the end. The Tic Bean is pale brown in colour but will darken with age if stored properly. Beans that are damp will turn black very quickly. The Tic Bean is grown mostly in Europe and is the foundation upon which all pigeon corn mixtures are based.

The water content of the Tic Bean is about fifteen per cent, whilst the protein and carbohydrate content are twenty-five and fifty per cent respectively. The bean contains about seven per cent fibre and only three per cent fat. There are approximately 1,350 calories per pound.

TARES

Tares are very much like miniature Maple Peas in appearance, and are grown on plants that belong to the vetches family. They are the usual brown in colour although there is a variety which may appear more grey than brown. The nutritional feeding value is very similar to that of the Maple Pea too. The water content is about thirteen per cent, the protein content about twenty per cent and the carbohydrate content sixty per cent. The Tare contains about six per cent fibre and two per cent water, the calorie count being 1,420 per pound.

BUCKWHEAT

Buckwheat is a poor food for pigeons and is not used in many mixtures, it is not a legume but comes from a variety of tall grass.

In appearance it is the shape of a triangular-based pyramid, in colour is a dull drab brown. The Buckwheat has a carbohydrate content of almost sixty per cent compared to a protein content of only twelve per cent. It carries a water per cent of fourteen which is high.

Perhaps the greatest drawback in feeding Buckwheat is that it has a high fibre content of twelve per cent and a low fat content of only two per cent.

BARLEY

This is a type of food that does not carry any real value at all because it has a high water content of about ten per cent, twelve per cent protein, and seventy per cent carbohydrate. For this reason it is used almost exclusively as a maintenance ration which means to say that it is used sparingly in winter when the birds are resting and just keeps the pigeon's body in a stable condition without becoming too fat. The fat content is very low at barely two per cent and the fibre content is almost six per cent which is very high. Pigeons usually have to be forced to eat barley but will soon learn what is required of them if the rations are kept on the small side. Barley has a calorie count of 1,405 per pound.

MAIZE

Maize is perhaps the most well known of all pigeon foods, it is present in almost every type of mixture.

There are quite a number of words to describe maize, such as: Indian Corn or Mealy Maize or Sweet Corn. It is in fact the true corn, all the others being merely grains of grasses or peas and beans as already described. Maize is grown all over the world and in fact it is the staple diet of many of the poorer people in poor countries.

In these places the maize is ground into flour and used to make flat cakes which are cooked in crude ovens or on hot stones. Maize can be best described as wedge-shaped, broad and flat.

The usual colour is either a deep golden orange or a yellowish orange. The colour depends entirely upon which type of maize is in question as there are several varieties. The commonest maize is called Plate Maize. Then there is Dent Maize, so called because it has a characteristic dent in its structure, then there is Flint Maize which has a hard brittle skin covering the kernel. Maize is very rich in carbohydrates and in fact carries a nearly seventy per cent content.

The protein content of maize is very low indeed at only ten per cent, and for this reason it should not be used *in excess* in pigeon food mixtures because the bird's body will store the carbohydrates that are not needed as fat. Maize is useful in building up fat reserves for long-distance racing pigeons which need to call upon rich reserves in order to keep going over their long and hazardous journey.

The pure fat content of maize is about average at three per cent, with little fibre at about two per cent and a water content of 15%. Because of its high carbohydrate content maize has a high calorie count of 1,506.

Too much maize will cause the birds to become too fat, which in turn will cause all kinds of problems such as egg-binding, and the inability of the racing bird to beat its sleeker, fitter competitors.

WHEAT

Wheat is present in almost every kind of pigeon food mixture. It is very nutritious because it contains wheat germ oil as well as an abundance of vitamins.

Good wheat is firm and plump, it is a golden yellow colour and without any kind of blemish. Bad wheat very often is thin and more of a pasty colour, it also has a distinct musty smell. Early harvesting is very often the cause of a bad crop of wheat, and therefore the grains have not had enough time to swell to their full capacity and ripen. English wheat is very often the victim of bad summers when the weather is wet for weeks on end, usually the signal for farmers to try and save what they can from their crop.

The protein content of wheat is about fifteen per cent, and the carbohydrate content about eighty per cent so you can see why it is such a valuable source of vitamins. The fibre content is low at two per cent and the fat content also below average at about one per cent.

Some pigeon fanciers are reluctant to feed their birds on new wheat because they say it causes diarrhoea and other related problems. Older wheat is much safer because the water content has had time to evaporate to a greater degree.

Storing Food

It is very important that the pigeon fancier has adequate facilities for storing his supply of food where it is free from damp and vermin. Nothing ruins pigeon corn more quickly than damp conditions; the grain soon becomes mouldy and therefore unfit for consumption.

Vermin, on the other hand, are a threat to the health of the pigeon fancier himself if their presence is not checked in its early stages. Mice can easily be eradicated with the use of traps and poison bait. Rats cannot be caught quite so easily without finding out where they are nesting, also the traps used in their capture are cumbersome. Rat poison is a very dangerous substance and can cause the death of a dog or cat if it is used without discretion.

Mice and rats, both, are disease carriers and should not be tolerated at any price. It is commonsense therefore that the containers used for corn should, if possible be gnaw proof. Such appliances are a bit on the expensive side but the fancier can rest assured that vermin will not reach the food and contaminate it. Most corn bins on the market are made from galvanised metal and will last the fancier a lifetime.

If the purchase of a corn bin is out of the question it is useful to be able to store the corn indoors, which means the use of a spare room or cupboard within the fancier's own house. Dustbins are very useful for a substitute corn bin; although they are not gnaw proof they are damp proof. Plastic dustbins can be purchased for a modest price. It is always better to store your food away from the loft for obvious reasons.

If however the fancier has no choice but to store his corn in or near the loft, there should be no holes in the building's structure where vermin can gain entry. Vermin traps and/or bait should always be present but in a place where they will do no harm to anything else.

When ordering food, allow for the fact that ½ cwt (25 kg) will last 24 pigeons 6-8 weeks.

How to feed

Feeding pigeons is an art in itself, it cannot be learnt quickly.

To the non-fancier this may sound a load of rubbish but it is nevertheless a fact. If pigeons are over-fed they become lethargic, they do not want to exercise, they sit about the loft all day with nothing to interest them. Fat pigeons will contract more diseases than pigeons that are fit. They will also be unable to breed as easily because the hens will become egg-bound. Egg-bound hens are those that accumulate layers of fat around their ovaries making the laying of the egg a difficult business. Fat pigeon hens are anyway less fertile than their slimmer sisters.

Pigeons that are underfed cannot build up a resistance to disease; they fall prey to the slightest malady. Because of their poor condition these diseases can easily turn into more serious problems such as Paratyphoid. Hungry pigeons are also lethargic and will not exercise properly as they should. They will forever be hanging about the loft looking for food, and if they have the opportunity they will go fielding where they can either be shot or pick up poison in the form of modern fertilizers.

From this it will be seen that a balance is required between the two extremes. To do this requires a little commonsense and an eye for detail. After feeding there should never be any food left in the hopper for more than an hour after feeding time. If there is food still present then it is clear that the birds are being overfed because they are eating their fill and leaving anything that is left. There are two points to watch here. Firstly, the pigeons will only be eating the grains that they prefer and this is not always what is good for them. Secondly, any food that is left in the hopper will soon become soiled and therefore become a health risk. Any food that is left over should never be left lying around.

The obvious answer here is to cut the food down, but the question is by how much? Well now, suppose we are faced with the problem of pigeons that always leave food at the end of feeding time. If the birds do not appear keen at meal times they are grossly overfed and their rations should be cut by at least one third for a couple of days. The effects of this will be startling; the birds will become as keen as a knife edge at mealtimes. From here we must now build them up until they are feeding at an acceptable level without being either too hungry or too full. The difference can be as slight as one handful of corn!

At feeding times watch the birds as they feed and when the second bird has finished feeding and gone to the water fountain for a drink it is a signal to the fancier to stop feeding. If this practice is carried on for a week it will be evident that the birds will become much more easy to manage. Feeding by hand in this way will also contribute to the pigeons' tameness whilst in the loft.

Another method of feeding pigeons is to hopper-feed them which entails the use of an automatic hopper which dispenses food at the rate at which it is being eaten. In other words the hopper should be able to maintain a level of food sufficient to the birds needs at all times. The only part the fancier plays in feeding is to ensure that the hoppers are always full. One would think that this method of feeding would overfeed the birds but surprisingly this is not true.

The hopper-fed pigeon will only take as much as it needs and will not fill its crop to bursting just for the sake of it.

There is another version of hopper-feeding which does not

require the use of an automatic hopper. The hopper must however be covered to prevent the contents becoming soiled. The hopper is filled and then left in front of the birds for a given period, say between the hours of four and six in the evening.

All feeding and watering utensils must be kept as clean as possible. Cleanliness is very important when feeding pigeons, and this is never more true than when feeding the birds straight onto the loft floor as is often the practice. Where this is done the floor must be scrubbed clean with a scraper and brush first. Failure to do this may result in the birds' picking up an infection that will soon spread right through the flock.

Stray birds must never, ever be fed with your own birds. Although they may look perfectly all right they may be carriers of such diseases as Coccidiosis which will prove fatal if not recognised in time.

Food hoppers should never be left lying around the loft floor whether they are empty or not. They should be scraped and brushed down after use and either hung or placed somewhere out of the way.

All feeding and watering appliances should be scrubbed every week in hot soapy water to which a disinfectant has been added.

It is possible to buy special detergents with disinfectant properties that are formulated especially for pigeon fanciers' use.

Whenever the drinking water is changed the bowl or trough should be rubbed round and rinsed to remove anything that may have accidentally fallen in. Healthy pigeons are always shedding bloom which is in fact a very fine dust. This bloom soon settles upon water and can often be seen as a fine film over the drinking water. The removal of this film is of course commonsense and it should be done as often as possible.

Water should be in front of the pigeons for twenty-four hours a day, but feeding times are different.

There are fanciers who give a light feed early in the

morning and a heavier feed at night. The more usual practice is to feed once per day at night. Restricting feeding to one meal per day simplifies feeding and also helps prevent overfeeding.

The use of small seeds in the morning is quite permissible (provided it is not overdone) as these mixtures contain seeds that are heating to the body (see page 79). Small seeds are often used in trapping mixtures which are used to lure the birds into the loft after exercise.

4

Breeding

The breeding season is the part of the year that the pigeon fancier looks forward to throughout the long winter months. During this time the birds are resting; they are not very active and their rations are kept to a level which should ensure that they are not carrying any extra weight.

The breeding season however sees a complete reversal of all this. The birds gradually become more aware of the opposite sex, the cocks start driving and the hens begin to eye the nest box with a view to making it a permanent home. The pigeon's breeding season extends from the beginning of March through to the end of July. The only exceptions to this are the stock birds and the fancier who races his pigeons on the widowhood system (see page 70). The stock birds are mated about the beginning of February so that their youngsters will be well advanced through the moult when the young bird racing season begins.

The widowhood birds are bred from at this time also, in order to get the first nest weaned as quickly as possible. This allows the adult cocks to be taken away from their hens and installed into the widowhood loft ready for the start of the Old Bird racing season, which usually begins about the first or second weekend in April.

The dangers of breeding so early in the year are that the weather can change quite suddenly. The fancier may find that although one day he can be basking in the sun the next day he may well be up to his armpits in snow! Frost is the early breeder's worst enemy because, when the youngsters reach the age of ten days old, they are often left uncovered by their parents and easily catch a chill. Even worse, if they are left uncovered overnight, they could freeze to death.

Really there is nothing better than a youngster that is born

47

around the end of April, because it grows up in a warm environment where it can enjoy the benefits of the longer days and sunshine.

Sound healthy youngsters grow up into sound healthy adults which is, after all, the aim of breeding in the first place.

Sexing Pigeons

Despite the various old wives' tales that are circulated amongst pigeon fanciers there is no fool-proof method of sexing pigeons merely by looking at them. There are cocks which look very much like hens and there are also hens which look very much like cocks. In general however the cock has a bolder face and head than the hen, and the cock's wattle over the beak is usually bigger and more wrinkled. There used to be an old saying that the cock has a rounded head whilst the hen has a flat head; this is fallacious.

The only real way to tell the sexes apart is to study them as they go about their business. The cock will usually have the deeper and more noisy call as he spins round and round in display to the hen. This display is termed driving and is in fact a form of courtship ritual.

The recessive red-coloured cock pigeon will also have black splashes over his feathers on the wings, tail and sometimes over the body.

The hen on the other hand has a call that is shrill and much shorter than that of the cock; she will parade in front of the courting cock by letting her wings hang down to touch the floor as she walks. She will hold her head erect and take little light steps as she runs from the advancing cock. Hens are usually much more finer in the face than are cocks, the beak is thinner and more pointed, the eye cere (the fleshy skin around the outside of the eye) is fine, and the wattle small and smooth. There are occasions when a hen may take on the actions and appearance of a cock, and it is not uncommon for spare hens to mate amongst themselves. (When two hens 'mate' one of them assumes the role of the male and the other will lay infertile eggs. Spare hens will only lay if they are mated, either by a cock, or a hen acting as a cock. They will not lay constantly as do chickens.) Likewise this can also happen to cocks the only difference being that when two cocks pair up there is an absence of eggs in the nest.

Youngsters are often very difficult to sex right up to their becoming mature adults. In this manner many a young cock has been mistaken for a hen and raced accordingly. It does not make any difference, and in actual fact it is far safer to race these birds of doubtful sex as hens because, if they are placed with the cocks and they are actually hens, they will not be able to fight off the attentions of so many members of the opposite sex and can become frightened.

Pairing up

It is best to keep the sexes separated during the winter, as this stops them from breeding and helps the moult.

It is best if they cannot see each other at this time.

In the Spring the fancier decides which cock he wishes to pair with which hen. Those birds that have been paired together before should not present the fancier with any problems. However there are always the awkward ones which seem to prefer the hen or cock of a completely different pair and so upsetting all the plans which have been so carefully formulated. We will deal with these misfits a little later but first we must pair up those birds that will present us with little or no trouble. Each pair must be allocated a nest box that has a door that can be shut and fastened to keep the birds in their rightful box. Each nest box should contain a nest pan or bowl into which has been placed a handful of sawdust.

Also it is a wise precaution to instal an ordinary household brick, so that the hen of the pair can escape from the constant attentions of the cock for a few minutes. If the hen has no refuge it may happen that the cock will scalp his hen by pecking at her head in his efforts to attract her attention. It is attention to small details like this that make all the difference between a good breeding season and a bad one.

The cock and the hen of each chosen pair are put into their

respective nest box and locked in together for a few hours. This can be done overnight. The first pair are then allowed their freedom within the loft but still able to enter their nest box. All the rest of the pairs are checked to ensure that everything is in order and they are fed and watered in their boxes. The first pair are then studied carefully to ensure that they are mated and are compatible. When they can find their way back into their nest box they are locked in again, and the next pair are then allowed their freedom and these too are carefully watched to ensure that everything is in order and that they too can find their way back into their own nest box. This method is repeated until all the pairs have been allowed their freedom and been mated and they know where their nest boxes are located.

Once all the pairs have mated, they can all be let out in the loft together, although there will usually be the odd cock who will persist in fighting all his fellow inmates.

This pigeon will delight in emptying all the nest boxes in his immediate neighbourhood, he will fight all-comers and will win with ease. The rogue bird will then establish a reputation amongst the flock for being aggressive and all the other birds will flee from his constant fighting. Many fanciers will dispose of such a trouble-maker out of hand, but if he is a valuable bird then the answer is much more difficult.

It is better to lock the trouble-maker and his mate in their nest box for a few days until all the other pairs are well settled in their respective nest boxes. Then the other cocks will put up a fight for their own rights and in some cases defeat the rogue cock.

Another slightly different method of pairing up the pigeons is to keep them locked in their nest boxes until the hens have laid their first egg. This method has two advantages in that the pairs are more easily settled to their nest boxes and the parentage of the resultant youngsters can be guaranteed. The only disadvantage with the latter method is that larger than normal nest boxes are required to enable the pair to mate properly.

Egg Laying

The first egg will usually be laid within ten days of the pair first mating, usually in the early evening. Pigeon eggs are about three to four centimetres long and white in colour. The first egg is not incubated properly, but the hen or cock may sit on it for a short time. The second egg is laid on the day but one after the first egg. Incubation proper begins in earnest at this time and the pair will settle down on the eggs.

It will be found that the hen of the pair will sit from early evening until around eleven o'clock the following day at which time she will be relieved by her partner. The cock will sit from around eleven in the morning until early evening. During incubation the pair should be disturbed as little as possible otherwise this will make them nervous and broken eggs could be the result.

Incubation lasts about eighteen days from the laying of the second egg. The colour of the eggs takes on a change as incubation progresses, they become a bit transparent and look darker inside. Infertile eggs, or clear eggs as they are more often called, remain opaque all through incubation, but should not be removed as this might cause the hen to desert the other egg. The period from when the young pigeon or squab begins to tap its way out of the egg until it has emerged and is fully dry is called 'the Hatch'. It is a very critical time during the young bird's life. The perfect hatch is when both birds hatch together, and the parents take the halves of the egg shells away from the nest.

As the time for hatching approaches the parents should be left strictly alone, but on the day of hatching all that is required is that the sitting bird be lifted up with one hand and the nest inspected. If the squabs have hatched but the egg shells not removed they should be taken away by the fancier. If, however, only one egg has hatched the unhatched egg can be removed and inspected. It will usually be found that the chick has made a small hole or dent in the shell but seems to be having a struggle to gain its freedom from the egg. The fancier can assist by chipping some of the shell away and then leaving the chick to do the rest itself.

If there is still no improvement after an hour or two the youngster can be assisted further until it is free. It will usually be found that these late hatchers are slightly smaller than their stronger brothers or sisters. If the difference in size is marked it might be better to dispose of the weakling and give the lone youngster a better start in life.

The young pigeon feeds on the yolk of the egg during incubation and can live for about twenty-four hours without being fed by its parents. Just before the eggs hatch the parents begin to form soft food or pigeon milk in their crops. This substance is more of a curd than a true milk and is made by the inner wall of the bird's crop falling away to lie in the bottom of the crop.

When the squab has dried out and rested for twenty-four hours or so it will pester its parents for food by instinct. The adult pigeon will open its beak and the chick will insert its own tiny beak. The adult will then regurgitate the soft food into the youngster. At this time it is done very gently and it is a marvellous sight to see the parent pigeons treat the youngsters as though they were made of china and might break if too much pressure were exerted during feeding.

This state of affairs does not last for long however, because the squabs grow at an amazing rate. By the time they are three to four days old the youngsters will have their eyes open and they will have lost the 'egg tooth', which is the tool they use to break their way out of the egg shell at hatching time. The egg tooth merely fades away as the beak changes shape.

Young pigeons of about one week old are perhaps the most ugly young birds that God made. The head is very large and the beady eyes appear as though they are popping out of the head. The young pigeons' legs and feet are big also and when sitting in the nest the poor bird looks as if it is destined to remain ugly for the rest of its life.

At about seven days old the youngsters have to be ringed with identification rings that are issued by the appropriate racing union or the N.P.A. which is the show pigeon organisation. Some details of how to obtain rings can be found in the Appendix, p.119. The ringing of a young pigeon requires a steady hand that is both firm and yet gentle. The young bird is taken from the next box still sitting in the nest bowl, it should never be taken out of the bowl as it may catch a chill. The ring is placed over the toes of either foot with the first three toes facing forward and the rear toe facing back. The ring is pushed over the ball joint of the foot and the rear toe is gently pulled through so that the ring is then on the bird's leg. As the youngster grows, the joint will also grow, and then become too large for the ring to pass over it and fall off. Ringing must be done before the joint gets too big because, if the job is neglected and difficulty is met when ringing the youngsters, they can easily be hurt and in some cases crippled for life.

Young pigeons do not forget easily and, if hurt when ringing, will remember later in life when the fancier wants to handle them. In many instances they will become wild.

After ringing, a check should be made to ensure that the ring has stayed on the bird's leg. Any which have come off should be put back straight away as a delay may result in the joint becoming too big as just described. Young pigeons during the nestling stage should never at any time be taken from the nest and handled. The result of such silly action will be a fret mark across the feathers when they have fully grown. This fret mark is in fact a weakness in the feather and, in show pigeons, will be marked against the bird when the judge makes his choice.

The ring number of the youngster should be recorded in the stud book so that an accurate account can be kept of the pedigree. Records such as this are better in black and white; never trust your memory in such matters because you will always forget something. The young pigeons should now be left to grow unhindered, they should not be disturbed and certainly never handled. It is very tempting to take the young from the nest and have a good look at them, but the fret marks as mentioned earlier will result and possibly the ruin of a youngster's chances for that year anyway, whether it be in the show pen or in the racing basket.

When the youngsters are twenty-one days old they will begin to peck at their own food although at this age they may not be able to manage to eat any of it. From the age of one week old the youngsters should be provided with a pot of corn once in the morning and once at night. The young at this age will not be able to take advantage of this themselves. The parent will feed the youngsters by regurgitation.

Young pigeons should never be allowed to go hungry for very long as it will weaken their constitution. The food pot should always be topped up as soon as it becomes empty, especially as the youngsters reach twenty-one days old.

As the young pigeons grow they will become more adept at eating and will emulate their parents in pecking at the corn provided in the pot. At twenty-eight days old the youngsters should be eating with confidence and at least half-filling their crops themselves.

It is at this age that they should be weaned or taken away from their nest and put into the young bird loft. Having a separate compartment or loft at this stage is very important. Young pigeons that are left to roam in the same compartment as the old birds will be bullied. This bullying can become very serious indeed with the result that many youngsters are scalped by pugnacious older birds, especially yearling cocks.

The young bird loft or compartment is a haven for these youngsters which, when placed there, will grow on undisturbed. For the first day or two the newly-weaned youngsters should be fed twice per day, once in the morning and once at night. At feeding time the corn tin should be rattled as a signal to the youngsters that it is feeding time. In racing pigeons this is a signal that they will remember all their lives and sometimes the quickness of their response will determine whether they are first or second on race day.

Once the youngsters have eaten and walked away from the food they should be shown where to find the water. The bird should be held in the hand and the pigeon's head lightly dipped into the water. Some will drink at the first attempt; others will not, but it is amazing just how quickly young pigeons learn how to drink. All that is usually necessary is for their beaks to be dipped two or three times.

By the time the youngsters are five to six weeks old their daily feed should be cut down to one meal per day. This is done in order to gain control of them and also to tame them and steady them in readiness for what is to come in the initial stages of their training.

Young show pigeons should be allowed to sleep overnight in the show pen in order that they can familiarise themselves with its interior. Likewise young racing pigeons should spend a night in the training basket so that they are familiar with it before training for racing begins in earnest.

It is very important indeed that the fancier gains the confidence of his youngsters. If they are frightened of him they will be difficult to train at a later stage. Wild youngsters will never give of their best whether it be in the show pen or in the racing basket, they are a nuisance in the loft making all the other inmates nervous.

Young birds are controlled through their stomachs and so they should be fed accordingly, never too much and never too little but just enough to keep them 'on their toes'.

Hand-feeding is a good way of taming youngsters that are a little too wild and independent. It is a good plan to sit on the loft floor with the corn tin and allow the youngsters to run all over you. In this way they will quickly learn that you are not to be feared but rather that you are a source of food and in fact you are their friend.

Cleaning out the loft whilst the young birds are present is another method of taming them and getting them used to your presence. You should never tiptoe around the loft but on the other hand you shouldn't charge around like a bull in a china shop either.

Youngsters that are to be pen trained should be placed where there is some kind of noise and movement. The ideal place is in the fancier's own house; although other members of the household might object to this it is nevertheless good pen training and will give the young birds some idea of what they might expect at a small show.

5

Racing Pigeons

The modern racing pigeon is a bird that has been modelled by man into the fastest pigeon on earth. The racing pigeon is often referred to as the greyhound of the sky; it is sleek of feather, and well muscled to do the job for which it was bred.

Nobody knows exactly from which species or varieties of domestic pigeon the racer was evolved, but educated guesses say that the Old English Carrier was instrumental in its make up. Others state that the Antwerp was used, also the Dragoon. In fact it was probably a combination of all these breeds which saw the rise of the racing pigeon.

Certainly pigeon racing began somewhere in Belgium, where today the sport enjoys an almost fanatical following.

In the U.K., there are records to show that pigeon racing was a popular sport in the late 1800's and the early part of the 1900's. In this era there are such legendary names as Gurnay, Logan, Stanhope, and Bricoux and Barker. These men were the pioneers of pigeon racing; they bred pigeons for the sole purpose of receiving great pleasure in seeing their birds home from hundreds of miles away.

Unknown to these men at the time, they were in fact creating the first forms of racing pigeon. As the birds got better and better so too the race points were situated further and further afield until pigeons were finding their way home from as far afield as Barcelona and other areas of northern Spain. The man who could breed a bird to fly such a distance was a hero, and even today it is a wonderful feat and deserves the acclaim that it receives. As the different fanciers developed their pigeons they began to breed a family or strain of birds that were typical in appearance, and family traits started to appear. These differences were mostly connected with colour although the type of a pigeon often gave away evidence of its family background and ancestry.

Over the years there have been many different strains of racing pigeon but the ones that have survived are the ones that have stood the test of time, and produced more race winners than the rest. From these old strains newer strains have evolved, but really they are basically all the same. For instance a fancier can select certain birds from one strain and cross them with birds from an entirely different strain; the resultant youngsters are then tested in the races and those that either win or show the most promise are then bred from in turn and the whole family is blended with the result that a new strain evolves.

Although it sounds very easy and almost foolproof it is in fact very, very, difficult to gain a satisfactory end result. Many fanciers give up and then start afresh with the consequence that they again make the same mistakes. Building up a successful strain involves years and years of hard patient work. In fact one of the most recent strain makers, the late Pierre Dordin named his residence and lofts 'Villa Patience'.

Most racing pigeon fanciers of today can select their prospective strain from quite a number that are advertised in the weekly fancy press.

There are a number of ways that the new fancier can start with racing pigeons and all have their advantages and disadvantages.

Perhaps the most common method is to go to a successful fancier in your local neighbourhood and ask to buy some late breds from him. These will be birds that were bred too late for racing in the year of their birth. These birds should be left to grow on and mature until they are at least nine or ten months old before they are mated up and bred from.

The youngsters that are bred from the late breds can then be put in the basket and raced. In the same way, stock birds that are proven to breed good birds can be purchased and bred from, but this is usually a very expensive method of starting up, because proven stock birds are not cheap and are not offered for sale as often as the untried late bred. Whether late bred or stock bird, the basics of pigeon keeping should be studied beforehand. It is no use buying expensive birds if they cannot be looked after properly.

If late breds are purchased it is best to settle them to your loft whilst they are still very young. First of all the fancier should begin to get the birds used to him by hand feeding them once per day. Each time they are fed, the corn tin should be rattled as a signal to the birds that it is feed time. If the birds are fed at the same time every day they will soon learn that, when the fancier enters the loft at that time, they will be fed.

When the birds are reasonably used to this routine the loft doors or trap can be opened to allow the birds their freedom. It is better to do this just before feeding time when the birds will be very attentive and looking for their daily ration of corn. Never at any time force the birds out of the loft. Quietly retire to a safe distance where you can observe their antics without disturbing them. At first the birds will be a bit wary and perhaps not venture very far, they will probably just fly onto the front of the loft and stand looking around their new surroundings; this is fine and it is better if you can now entice them back into the loft by shaking the corn tin and calling them. Once they are all safely inside the loft the trap can be shut and the youngsters fed as normal.

This exercise can be repeated every evening until the birds begin to feel their wings and venture into the air. This is the most frightening time of all (not for the pigeons but for the fancier), as it is the time when the moment of truth arrives. At first the young late breds will be all over the sky in their first attempts to fly.

Gradually, however, they will learn to fly together in a group and will delight in turning and twisting as they zoom over the loft in circles. It is at this time that the largest number of young birds are lost, so great care should be taken to ensure that they are not left out too long, as this will give them the opportunity to travel too far too fast. Once all the birds have landed on the loft they should again be called in and fed as before.

Ideally the birds should land either on the loft roof or on the landing board in front of the loft.

All pigeons, young and old, need regular exercise, and should be let out daily for an hour or so before being called back into the loft.

Stock Birds

Stock birds, as explained earlier, are birds that have proved themselves either on the road or in the breeding pen. They cannot be treated the same as the late bred, because they will be adult birds that have flown to another loft and therefore, if allowed their liberty, will return to their former home.

Stock birds *can* be settled to a new environment but it takes a great deal of patience. If the bird's former loft is some distance away, failure means that it will be quite expensive to retrieve a wayward pigeon.

It is therefore better not to allow the stock bird its liberty. This may sound a bit drastic but in reality it is merely a method of ensuring that the bird has everything that it requires to breed some youngsters for its new owner. Therefore it is a good idea to build some sort of aviary, in which the stock bird can take the fresh air and bathe, without the risk of the bird being lost.

The aviary is merely a frame over which wire netting is stretched. The floor should ideally be of concrete or soft earth that can be dug over in order to clean it out. The roof of the aviary should be open to the elements so that both sunshine and rain can penetrae. There is nothing like rainwater for putting a shine or bloom on a pigeon's feathers; the birds will love to sit out whilst it is raining and bathe to their heart's content. This can also be applied to sunshine because pigeons love to sunbathe whenever they are allowed the opportunity.

The wire netting that is used to cover the aviary should be 19 gauge ($\frac{1}{2}''$ by $\frac{1}{2}''$) to deter cats. The neighbouring cat will be the fancier's greatest enemy and there is no sense in giving it an expensive free meal through lack of detail on the fancier's part.

The size of the aviary will depend entirely upon the number of birds that it will house. An aviary size of three cubic metres will accommodate only one pair in comfort and therefore if this space is used as a guide the amount of space should be increased pro rata with each additional pair of birds that are kept.

It is better to site the aviary on the side of the loft that is visible from the house if the loft is one that is sited in the fancier's garden so that the cat menace can be checked. If the loft is away from the house it would be an advantage to site the aviary on the side of the loft where the sun shines for most of the day. As well as benefiting the birds, the ultra-violet rays from the sun will also kill any germs that may be present in the birds' droppings. If possible vermin such as sparrows and starlings should be discouraged from entering the aviary as they are carriers of avian diseases and parasites.

Old Bird Training and Racing

Many fanciers will say that the racing of their old birds is the highlight of the racing year and that they are not so much bothered about racing the young birds. It is true to say that old bird racing requires much more skill in finding out which bird will perform well in which type of weather and in what kind of wind. There is also the added complication of what is termed the bird's 'best nesting position'. This is the state of affairs the bird finds itself in when it is entered into a race; for instance it may be incubating eggs, or it may be feeding a large or small youngster.

If a certain pigeon will home faster when it is sitting on eggs that are about ten days old then it would certainly be an advantage to try and get the bird into this position for a certain race, or to race it from the distance from which it usually performs best. Young bird racing does not require such complicated permutations because the birds merely fly to the loft and their food. Young bird racing is therefore much more a matter of good luck than good judgement.

It is a common saying in pigeon racing circles that races are won and lost at the home end, and this is very true indeed. It will be evident that the fancier has to have a method of trapping his birds that is both very fast and efficient. There are two basic methods, firstly there is the trap which is a hinged door over the landing board or let as it is sometimes described. The basic idea is that the bird will land on the board or let and then drop through the trap into the loft.

This method has the disadvantage that sometimes the birds which arrive home from a race are very nervous and therefore they are wary about entering the loft at the first attempt. The trap sometimes gives the bird the jitters and it will waste valuable seconds whilst it makes up its mind to enter the loft. The advantages of this system are that the race bird can enter the loft without the danger that any of the inmates can escape whilst the bird is coming in from the race.

The other method of trapping that is used in the U.K. is that of the open door. This entails the use of wide doors along the front of the loft that are either hinged or are fastened to a sliding system. The race bird will therefore either pitch straight into the loft interior, or it will land on a platform outside. The platform outside the loft is usually about one metre wide and as long as the loft itself. The open door method is much favoured, but it requires the fancier to have much more control over his birds. Whichever type of trapping system is used the birds must be thoroughly used to it and be able to enter the loft confidently.

Liberties can be taken with old birds that can never be taken with young birds; for instance the distance of the first training toss will generally be further than it would be for young birds. Old birds are considered to be able to negotiate training tosses because they have more experience.

Basketing
Pigeons should never be handled roughly at any time, but it is particularly important that they are not handled roughly when they are put into the basket.

As stated earlier, pigeons will always remember an upsetting experience and the sight of the basket will surely upset a bird if it connects this with rough handling. As each pigeon is caught up it should be soothed and calmed in the hand before attempting to put it into the basket. Many fanciers make the mistake of just dropping the pigeon into the basket but it will be found that the poor bird simply lands on its head! Hardly conducive to good relations!

Each pigeon should be placed into the basket so that it can put its feet down first. Pigeons are quarrelsome creatures by nature and will fight and bicker in the basket. Why this should be the case it is difficult to say, because there is no territorial advantage to be gained by pushing one another about. The basket should be kept in the horizontal position at all times; again it will be upsetting to the pigeons should the basket be swung about and all the inmates pushed down one end and seconds later sent scurrying down to the other end.

One more important point to remember is never to overcrowd pigeons in the basket. Birds that are crammed into a basket feel very uncomfortable and if involved in fights within the basket will be unable to escape. If your basket is described as a ten bird basket, try to remember this and do not be tempted to squeeze fifteen birds into it. Before placing the basket into the car or whatever means is used for transportation, check that all straps are secure and all buckles are fastened properly. The pigeons should be transported to their destination in a quiet orderly manner. It is no use taking care during basketing and then driving like a lunatic and upsetting the birds on the journey.

The first training toss should be about five miles from home, in the general direction of the first race point.

Releasing

Once at the first training point the basket should be unloaded from the car and placed on the roof of the car or some convenient place off the ground. This is to prevent dust being blown into the basket and also keeps the birds away from any passing dogs.

The pigeons should now be left for about ten minutes to settle down and take stock of their bearings. It has been proved that, if birds are released straight away on arrival at the training point, they will circle the spot for quite some time and will take a long time to clear. On the other hand those that are allowed to take stock and gather their wits after the journey will not circle as many times and will begin their journey home that much faster. When choosing a training site keep well away from buildings, trees, telephone wires and power cables. Many injuries are caused to racing pigeons because their owners neglected to check that the flight path is clear before releasing the birds. The flight path does not just mean the direction in which the basket is facing; it also means all round the site. This is because the birds will often swing round with the wind and begin their journey home in the opposite direction!

After the appointed time has elapsed the strap which holds the front flap secure should be unbuckled in readiness for the liberation.

The basket flap is now lowered and the birds allowed their liberty. On no account should the pigeons be frightened out of the basket but at the same time ensure that none are left behind when the leaders make their exit. All the fancier needs to do is to put his hand at the rear of the basket and it should be enough to encourage the stragglers to leave.

Once into the air the pigeons will climb and gain height in order to see where they are and get their bearings. Should the birds circle for a long time do not be alarmed as this will often happen even after the best of liberations. It may seem that the birds have gone in the opposite direction but really all they have done is fly in a huge circle and they will soon reappear on the right track. It is also fairly likely that pigeons which have never been trained before will take some considerable time to reach home. This is not unusual and really it is good for their education as they will have covered quite an area of ground and will remember this on subsequent training tosses.

From now on the training tosses will be increased in distance as the birds gain more and more experience.

From five miles we can progress to ten miles and then on to twenty or thirty miles. It is often said that the first few tosses are the most important as they teach the pigeon the basics of what is expected of it later on. The frequency of the training tosses will depend entirely on the cost of travel. If the birds can be sent with a friend on his regular business so much the better; if the fancier can take them himself then this is really the ultimate because he or she will know the weather conditions at the release point. The weather plays a very important part in pigeon racing and whenever possible the weather forecast should be listened to before making a liberation. Pigeons will fly through rain and high winds, but thunderstorms and mist will send them astray. On a clear day with a tail wind the birds will fly at 60 m.p.h. The weather forecast gives the experienced fancier a way of estimating how long the birds will take to cover the distance. Once the pigeons really know their way home from say twenty to thirty miles away they should be taken on training tosses merely to sharpen up their muscles.

Single Up Tosses

Single up means that the birds are released one at a time instead of in a flock. This system has the advantage that it makes the birds think for themselves. Pigeons that are always released in a flock develop a tendency to rely on the leaders to show them the way home and, when they become split up, are lost. The single up therefore teaches the pigeon to be independent and think for itself. Any bird that does not possess the homing instinct to its fullest extent will soon be shown up, mostly by its absence at the loft when the fancier returns home.

Single up tosses should be carried out at fifteen minute intervals and therefore it takes some time to release a basketful of pigeons. The rewards far outweigh the disadvantage of time taken, because the fancier will know that his birds have the ability to fly on their own and think for themselves when faced with a difficult situation.

If the birds are released any sooner than fifteen minute intervals, they will meet up with each other in the air and defeat the object of the exercise.

Trapping

Trapping is the method by which the returning racing pigeon enters the loft. The drop type trap and the open door method have been explained earlier and the advantages and disadvantages underlined. The open door method is without doubt the fastest method of the two and is more popular than any other. It is very interesting to note that the Belgians, who by the way are considered 'Aces' at the sport, do not use the open door method.

The Belgian, and indeed all continental fanciers use merely a small board and pop hole as a trap on their lofts.

Fig. 13 A Belgian loft

Look at the drawing of a typical Belgian loft (Fig. 13). Notice that the loft is in fact part of the fancier's house, something that would be very difficult to achieve in the U.K.

Council rules and regulations would never allow that sort of set-up. In the Belgian arrangement the returning bird has no option but to alight on the board from where its movement is either to fly off again, or to enter the loft. It is also most certain that the pigeon would enter the loft rather than fly off again, except if something happened to frighten it away.

None of the trapping methods are of any use without first teaching the bird to enter the trap as quickly as possible. Pigeons are controlled mainly through their stomachs therefore the bird has to be taught that on a given signal it must enter the loft and once inside it will receive food.

The training begins as soon as the young bird leaves the nest and begins to fend for itself. At each meal time the corn tin is shaken or the fancier whistles. This is the signal, and the hungry pigeon should respond to it straight away. As soon as the young bird begins to look for food at the onset of the signal it will never forget it. The only time that a negative response is received is when the bird is not hungry.

Therefore when pigeons are released from either a training toss or by taking part in a race, they should be reasonably hungry so that on their return to the loft they will not hang about on the loft roof but will enter as soon as possible. There are however some birds which are brilliant racers but will not trap on their return.

Nesting conditions

Nesting conditions merely means the stage of reproduction a particular bird is in at a given time.

In the case of the racing pigeon the best time is when the pigeon is keen and will be eager to return to its home loft.

There are no hard and fast rules to cover all pigeons; they are all individuals and therefore they will require different situations to make them keen. The racing pigeon fancier should above all be observant and notice when his birds are at their best. Once noted, this should be used to advantage and the bird encouraged to be in that particular condition for a certain race. Likewise, the fancier should note the distance at which his bird will perform at its best. The clever fancier will now combine the two and have his bird in the right nesting condition at the time it is entered for a race which will be from its best distance.

Driving

The driving position is when the cock bird is chasing his hen to nest. In other words he will be showing his hen that he is willing to get down to the serious business of breeding. A word of caution here. Young birds, especially yearlings are very headstrong at this time in their lives and will fly after anything resembling their own mate. It is foolish to send yearling cocks, that are driving their hen, to races because the cock will not race properly but fly after other hens on his way home and make a hash of the whole thing. Many, many yearlings are lost every year through their owners being thoughtless and sending them to races thus. Older birds that are more experienced will fly quite well in this position and come to no harm at all.

It should also be borne in mind that driving cocks use up a lot of energy whilst cavorting about and so they should not be raced from distances that might tax their stamina.

Sitting

This position includes the birds sitting on newly laid eggs right up to the day of hatching. It goes without saying that hens that are 'in egg', or, in other words, hens that are about to lay eggs, should never be sent racing. Egg laying is a strain on the body's resources in its own right without the bird having to exert itself in a race.

The best time to send pigeons racing whilst they are sitting on eggs is on the tenth day. This condition is important for two reasons. Firstly the birds will have settled nicely to the job of incubation, and they will be calm and collected. Secondly, the tenth day is about mid-way through the term of incubation and therefore the birds will begin to look forward to the day when the eggs hatch out. Only one of the pair is sent racing. The other stays at home and carries on incubating.

At the other extreme we can send birds racing that are due to hatch out their eggs. For the fancier with a small loft and a limited number of race birds this nesting position can be dangerous in that he could easily lose his bird and the other pigeon at home will desert the young. This is a very great danger and should be seriously considered before the bird is sent to the race. Another aspect of this condition is that the pigeon will carry 'pigeon milk' in its crop as the time approaches for the eggs to hatch out. Whether a racing pigeon is handicapped when it has a crop of soft food is a controversial matter and one which should also be considered.

Feeding

Feeding youngsters is considered to be a difficult task for the racing pigeon to accomplish while racing at the same time. The parent pigeon will sacrifice itself for the sake of its offspring. This sacrifice consists of giving up food to ensure that the young are well nourished. It is for this very reason that galley pots are used in the nest boxes. The pots should never be empty, to ensure that the parent pigeon has sufficient nourishment both for itself and its young. Pigeons that are feeding small youngsters and are raced from short distances should not suffer unduly. The bird that is feeding big youngsters and sent on a long distance race is at a very great disadvantage.

There is a saying in racing pigeon circles (as elsewhere) that you cannot burn the candle at both ends. So you cannot breed from your birds *and* compete in races with any great success. To some extent this is true, but it is a fact that the majority of fanciers in this country do burn the candle at both ends, and also there has to be a winner of the race. If every fancier in a club breeds as many young birds from his adults as he possibly can and still races them and wins, then he will be bound to say that breeding and racing can be combined.

The Natural System

This combination of breeding and racing is known as the 'natural system', which is the method of racing pigeons to their mates and their nests.

This has been the way pigeons have been raced for over one hundred years, and there have been some remarkable performances by pigeons raced this way. There is however the disadvantage that the birds cannot all be available for racing every week of the racing calendar. Pigeons that are driving or feeding big youngsters are better left at home as explained earlier. For natural racing therefore the fancier has to have quite a large team in order to compete every week. The fancier with a small team who raced his birds every week would soon overwork his birds and they would be out of steam long before the end of the season.

The Widowhood System

This method of racing pigeons is not new, but it was seldom practised in its early years because not enough people took the time and trouble to study the method thoroughly.

The widowhood system begins in the same manner as the natural system with the rearing of one round of youngsters. Once these young birds have been weaned the sexes of the adult birds are separated and the hens are taken well away from the cocks. It is much better to have the hens out of earshot of the cocks otherwise the system will not work as well.

The hens should be placed in pens or boxes so that they cannot pair up amongst themselves. These birds are fed and watered in their pens during the whole of the racing season and are never allowed out.

The cocks on the other hand can either be left free in the loft or shut into their widowhood style nest boxes. The widowhood nest box differs from the regular type of nest box in that it has a centre division or gate which divides the nest box in half. The cocks are sent away training and on their return they will find their respective mates waiting for them in their nest box. The pair are allowed perhaps half an hour with each other before the hen is removed and placed back in her own box.

The pairs whilst in the widowhood next box are separated by the gate and never come into bodily contact with one another.

Whilst the cocks are in the nest box alone the nest pan is inverted all the time, but as soon as the cocks are to be taken away to the training point the nest bowls are turned over to their rightful position, as a signal to the cock that when he returns home his hen will be waiting for him.

Some cocks adapt very well to this new style of racing and seem to enjoy it. Other cocks will fret for their hens and never fly well enough to justify being kept on the system. Once the racing season is finished the widowers are allowed to rear a round of late breds to keep them happy. This has the effect

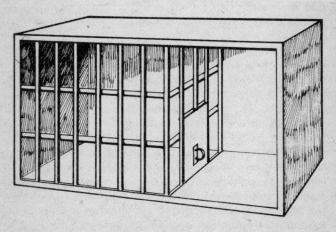

Fig. 14 Widowhood nest box

that it satisfies the homely hen and at the same time calms the highly strung giddy cock. Both these actions put the birds into the right frame of mind and then they will moult properly with no problems.

It was at first stated that the widowhood system required a lot more room and attention than the tried and tested natural system. The hens certainly do require more room as they have to have pens of their own.

The cocks can remain in the racing loft as normal. The time spent cleaning out the birds can actually be reduced, because the hens are in their boxes and can be stood on sheets of paper which only have to be changed once per day. If the cocks are kept in the widowhood nest box they too can be kept on paper and again easily cleaned once per day.

The widowhood hens are never raced and therefore it is often considered a waste of good racing birds. This is very true, but as the saying goes 'You cannot have your cake and eat it'. It is also true that pigeons raced on the widowhood system have to be of a strain that will adapt to this type of racing. In the same vein the food that these birds receive has to be of a type that is rich in carbohydrates for plenty of energy. The widowhood racing pigeon is in fact a sprint racer that will fly as fast as it possibly can for a given distance. The bird itself is bred for the job of flying fast for a short time. If these widowers were sent perhaps five hundred miles they could never hope to put up the same kind of performance. The widower's wing is very short in comparison to that of the long distance racer; the bird is short and wide in build, well-muscled and powerful.

Young Bird Training

Young bird racing is not the same as old bird racing in that the young birds are raced to the loft and their perch and not their mate. This does not mean to say that early bred youngsters cannot be paired up and raced as old birds. They can. Usually however the young bird remains in the young bird loft and is treated exactly the same as the rest of its comrades.

Young bird training begins from the day the youngsters are weaned. They are first of all taught the signal for feeding time, and are placed outside the loft in order to get used to seeing the exterior. Also they must learn the way into the loft. They will do this, as they will do most things, by following the example of others.

Young birds that are placed outside for the first time should not be strong enough on the wing to be able to fly around the loft. The danger from prowling cats is obvious and therefore a watchful eye should be kept on them. Once the youngsters are entering the loft as soon as they are called they need never be put out by hand again. The old birds should be given their exercise first and, when they are about to drop onto the loft, the young bird section can be opened.

The youngsters should now be left to fly out of the loft themselves without any help from the fancier. It will be surprising just how quickly the young birds find their way about and in no time at all they will be coming out into the open with confidence. At this stage the youngsters will not fly but merely sit about the loft enjoying the fresh air and sunshine. The time will come however when one of them will take to the air and fly away. It is handy to have an old bird or two on the loft with the young birds to act as a steadying influence on them. Once youngsters get into the air for the first time they can become quite giddy and drunk with power. Their new-found freedom seems to have a peculiar effect on the youngsters as they zoom across the sky in big wide circles.

It will take a number of flights such as this before the birds settle down and begin to fly in a group as the adults are apt to do.

Many youngsters are lost off the loft at this stage and so their freedom should be restricted to perhaps one hour at evening.

If youngsters are released early in the morning and they are not hungry they will begin to run, which is a term used to denote that they will stray from their home territory. Young birds have been known to run for up to four hours at a time and to cover an area of about forty miles radius from their loft. This type of thing is very educational and helps to tone up the muscles. However, if the young birds get mixed up with old birds that are training there is the very real danger that they will be taken much too far from their home and subsequently they will become lost. It is a terrible feeling to have your young bird team return from such a run in dribs and drabs with many of them missing at the end of the day. This sort of thing can be avoided if precautions are taken.

Once the young birds are beginning to run in this manner it is time they are introduced to the training basket.

One night they should be placed into the basket and whilst there they should be fed as usual. The water trough should be provided and the youngsters shown where it can be found.

The young birds are left in the basket all night and then released in the morning into the loft. If this procedure is carried out two or three times the birds will soon realise that there is nothing to fear from the basket and they will soon settle down in it when they are taken for their first training toss. Before training actually begins it is a good idea to put all the youngsters in the basket and release them a short distance away from the loft so that they fly from the basket straight onto the loft. The first time that the basket flap is opened the youngsters will walk out looking bewildered. If the exercise is repeated often enough the youngsters will soon learn to fly straight out of the basket.

As soon as basket training is completed the young birds can begin their training in earnest. By this time the colour of their eyes will have begun to change from a dark nondescript type of colour to eyes that show signs of a true coloured circle.

On the day that the young birds are to be taken for their first training toss they should be hungry. It is better then to take the young birds during the early evening just before their normal feeding time. As with the old birds the basketing of the birds should be done in a quiet orderly manner with no fuss. Frighten your young birds now and they will become basket shy and panic every time they see the basket brought into the loft. Once inside the basket the young birds should be transported as quickly as possible to their first release point about one mile away from the loft. If the young birds have been running well they will have passed this point many times before and so they will be familiar with it. The birds should be given time to settle down and then released. If the early basket training has been successful the young birds will fly straight out of the basket and form into a tight bunch as they circle the release point.

It is a fact that the birds will take a long time before they arrive at the loft. Nobody knows why this should be so but almost every young bird team will take ages in finding their way home from the shortest toss.

On these early tosses it is a very good idea to include an old bird or two to steady the youngsters and also to show them the way home. The inclusion of the old bird is merely a precaution against the young birds losing their heads and beginning to run instead of getting down to the task of finding their way home. If the fancier goes straight back to the loft he will find that he has beaten his young birds back and then preparation can be made for their arrival. The loft can be opened up and the corn tin half filled. As soon as the young birds make their appearance in the sky over the loft, the corn tin should be shaken and the birds called down.

It is good practice to call the youngsters into the loft as soon as they arrive, as it prevents the formation of any bad habits that they might otherwise develop if they were allowed to sit about on the loft roof. As soon as they are all in the loft they should be fed.

Training tosses from now on should be regular and the distance increased periodically. A week or two before the first young bird race, the youngsters should be coming from a forty-mile toss with ease and in good time. There will of course be the inevitable losses because no matter how well-bred our foundation stock might be, there will always be the birds that are below par and therefore not good enough to withstand the very hot competition that exists in pigeon racing today. This applies to the bird that looks as though it could beat allcomers; it might be superbly bred and have the looks of the exhibition racing pigeon. Once in the basket the story is entirely different and such a bird is often lost at the first training toss some distance from the loft. The basket is the best pedigree of all, it soon sorts out the weaklings and the riff-raff.

Once young birds are racing well they should be kept going as much as possible without being subjected to hard races week after week. Race young birds with their future in mind. In this respect it is better to split your young bird team into two and race one lot one week and the other lot the next week. In this way you are not asking the same birds to perform week after week and therefore asking too much of them whilst they are still learning.

Racing Equipment

Every fancier must have certain equipment before he or she can begin to race pigeons seriously. Most of this equipment is quite expensive but cheap materials never last very long and give a very unsatisfactory performance. Buy the best quality you can afford.

The Training Basket

The basket is a basic piece of equipment that no fancier can be without. There are various sizes on the market and of course the bigger the basket the more expensive it will be. However, it is wise to buy the biggest basket that your pocket will allow. Even though at the time of purchase there may not be very many birds in the loft, it will not always remain that way. If a basket with a central partition can be bought so much the better as this will allow the transportation of cocks and hens together without their being mixed up.

The training basket should be looked after if it is to remain in good condition. Cleaning out the basket is a job that often gets neglected. The result can be a build-up of bacteria which will infect the birds that are placed in it. Additionally the basket should be scrubbed out annually, and the exterior varnished to make it weatherproof. All baskets are made from willow and therefore, if left in the open or in damp conditions, they will rot.

It is in the fancier's interests to find somewhere dry and warm in which to store the basket over the winter months when it is not in use. Too frequently the basket is either put under the loft or shoved into a corner of the garden shed where it is forgotten about and neglected until it is needed the next year. Often the bottom falls out after such neglect.

The Timing Clock

This is perhaps the most important item of equipment the fancier is ever likely to need. If bought new it will certainly be the most expensive. Before the fancier can race his pigeons he or she must have a timing device into which the arrivals of the racers are recorded.

There are two main types of timing clock in use (both in the U.K. and in Belgium) and they are the puncturing clock and the printing clock. The puncturing clock records the arrival of the pigeon by making a pin-prick on a paper dial within the clock. The printer will print the time of the arrival on a roll of paper, also within the clock.

The Puncturing Clock

This type of clock is perhaps the oldest type in use and it is also the most reliable. The clock itself is wound up with a key and two dials are placed on a flat plate. The first dial is that which denotes minutes and seconds. The seconds division is divided into tenths for decimal readings in the case of a close finish to a race. The hour dial is divided into twenty-four segments. Both dials are placed onto the flat plate and are held into position with a locking nut. Over the dials is a small arm which has a needle at the tip. After being set in unison with the club's master timer, from which all the other clocks are set, all the clocks are struck by moving a lever. This will bring down the arm onto the dial and the needle will puncture the dial giving the time the clock was set. By comparing the 'set' time with that of the master timer we can establish whether the clock is running fast or slow.

When the pigeon returns from the race its race rubber ring is removed from its leg and placed into a thimble of which there are two halves. When the two halves of the thimble are locked together they are placed in the first chamber of the clock and the lever is depressed as in setting the clock. The dial is again punctured showing the arrival time of the bird and at the same time the next chamber of the clock is brought round to the open position to enable the fancier to record the arrival of his second and subsequent birds. When the clock is taken back to the club headquarters on the night of the race, all the clocks are struck in unison at a given time and then they are opened.

The rubber rings are removed from the clock's chambers and their serial numbers are checked against those recorded on the competitor's race entry sheet.

The Printing Clock

The printing clock is really self-explanatory; it is a pigeon timer that prints the time of the bird's arrival on a roll of paper.

The paper roll within the clock runs across an inked ribbon and when the clock is struck upon closing it after setting, the time that the clock was set will appear in a glass window on the roll. When the bird returns from the race the thimble is pushed into the chamber in exactly the same manner as the puncturing clock, the bird's arrival is then also recorded on the roll and can be read through the glass window with ease. The printers can either be clockwork or the more modern types are run from dry cell batteries. This type of clock is often sealed by the club with a numbered metal seal, as an added security measure.

Velocities

The velocity is the speed of the returning racing pigeon calculated into yards per minute (y.p.m.). All competitors have their lofts located on a map by the club secretary. The position is then calculated into degrees, minutes and seconds until the exact loft location is pinpointed. The distance from the competitor's loft to the race release point is then calculated in miles and yards.

The pigeon's velocity can then be calculated by defining the amount of time it took to fly from the race point until the time when the thimble containing the bird's rubber ring is placed into the timing clock.

The pigeon with the highest velocity is then declared the winner. The actual calculations are complex, therefore the above explanation is merely in its simplest form to give the novice a rough idea of how the system works.

As to the speeds achieved by pigeons, these depend very much on the weather conditions as well as the length of the race. Obviously a strong tail wind will make for a fast race while a head wind will make for a slow race. Also, dull overcast days give a slow race, as do clear hot sunny days. The fastest races are on clear cool days. A fast race could be as fast as 2,000 y.p.m., whereas in a slow or steady race speeds could be as little as 800 y.p.m.

Certain strains are known as sprinters and these should be raced in the shorter races, while others can fly long distances and win.

All birds that compete in races should be wing-stamped which entails putting the fancier's or club's name and address on the flight feathers with an inked rubber stamp.

Pooling

This is the method of betting money on the fancier's own birds. The winner will take a proportion of the pool, with the later birds taking lesser proportions. The pools go up in stages of 5p, 10p, 25p, 50p, £1, £5, £10, etc. If, for instance, the winner is only pooled to 25p, then it cannot take a share of the higher pools because it has not been entered in those pools.

Clubs

Pigeon racing is organised in clubs and federations and further information should be available from your local club or from the RPRA (See P.118).

6
Exhibition Pigeons

The world of exhibition pigeons is perhaps not as well known as its counterpart the racing pigeon fraternity. There are in fact some thirty to forty varieties of exhibition pigeons that are shown regularly in the United Kingdom. Perhaps the best known of these exhibition varieties is the Fantail; this may be because they are such likeable little birds that are usually bred in the back-garden dovecot. These Fantails are used merely for ornament in the garden and as pets for the general household. The real exhibition Fantail is very beautiful indeed and will pose in the show pen to show off its arched tail and the gently sloping lines of its body. Almost all the breeds of exhibition pigeons were originally bred in other countries and imported into the United Kingdom many years ago.

Some breeds of fancy pigeon, as they are more often called, are in fact dual purpose breeds, which means that they are flown outside the loft and are also exhibited in the show pen. The most notable of these breeds are the Tipplers, Tumblers, and the Birmingham Rollers.

Feeding

Feeding fancy pigeons is a little different from feeding the racing pigeon. The fancy pigeon does not require so much body-building food as the racing pigeon, but it does require the type of food that will give it sleek plumage, bright eyes, and brightly coloured legs. These are attributes that the fancy pigeon requires if it is to get on in the show world. Oily foods are therefore very important, but it must be remembered that the foods that are rich in oils are also heating to the body. This means that they heat the blood, which could cause an early moult, a situation to be avoided as the bird will be uncomfortable if it loses too many feathers at once.

Because most of the fancy breeds are delicate and have small beaks they must be fed on grains that are not too large for them to eat. A fancy pigeon mixture will therefore contain a large amount of small seed.

A good fancy pigeon mixture might contain the following: Red and white dari, maple peas, small maize, linseed, groats, tares. It is folly to allow the birds to feed straight from the loft floor as this might stain the plumage making the bird useless for showing. A better plan is to use one of the hoppers or trays as described in Chapter 2, page 19. Birds that are nesting can be fed in their nest boxes by placing their food in little pots which are easily cleaned out after use.

Perches

The fancy pigeon will require the saddle or 'Vee' perch on which to settle. Box perches for exhibition pigeons are detrimental to the care of the birds' feathers. If box perches are used the bird above may easily soil the bird perched below. 'Vee' perches make this very unlikely if they are positioned correctly.

Nest boxes

The nest box for fancy pigeons will be the same as that used for the racing pigeon with the exception that the fancy pigeon might require a door size a little larger. The inside of the nest box should be kept very clean and sprinkled with sawdust every time it is cleaned out.

Baths

Baths, too, are very important for the exhibition pigeon. It cannot be stressed too strongly just how clean the plumage has to be kept at all times. Therefore the birds must have permanent access to a bath. The water should be changed regularly and an anti-pest solution added if required.

Aviaries

This is perhaps the most important piece of equipment

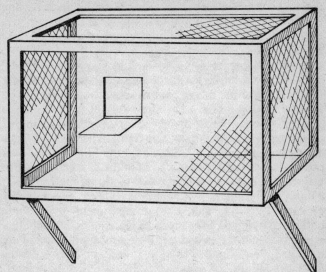

Fig. 15 A pigeon aviary. This one would suit fancy pigeons

concerned with fancy pigeon housing. Because the fancy
pigeon does not fly freely it has to have some kind of access
to sunshine and fresh air whenever it feels the inclination to
do so. The aviary should therefore be open to the birds at all
times during the day and only shut up at night.

Showpens

The fancier who wishes to compete in top class exhibitions
will require a set of show pens. These are wire cages in which
the pigeons are exhibited. It is a good plan to have a set of
these of one's own in which the birds can be trained before
they are actually exhibited. Nothing detracts from a good
fancy pigeon more than wildness in the show pen.

Show pens can be purchased through adverts contained in
the fancy press, and although they are not particularly cheap

they are an investment that will last the fancier for many years.

Show Baskets

The birds are transported to the shows in specially designed show baskets. On the outside these baskets look very much like the racing pannier except that there are no gaps around the sides. The show basket is divided into separate compartments by divisions of either sacking or canvas walls stretched on a wire frame. The compartments are long and narrow to ensure that the birds cannot turn round once they have been placed in the basket. If the bird was to be allowed enough room to turn round it could damage its feathers after they have been painstakingly prepared by the fancier. Each compartment of the show basket has a hinged lid of the same material as the walls; this prevents the bird from trying to escape by jumping out of the top.

Preparation For Showing

Before an exhibition pigeon can stand any chance of gaining an award in the show pen it has to be made ready for the occasion. Some birds will require much less preparation than others. To illustrate this point we can take the case of the Roller versus the Fairy Swallow. The Roller will only require that it be clean in feather and have a good bloom to the feathers, the wattle should be chalked and the legs washed.

The Fairy Swallow will have to be bathed with great care paying particular attention to the feathered legs and feet.

The amount of preparation required to get a bird fit for showing is a very important consideration when choosing which variety to keep. If you are the type of person who likes fiddling around with delicate operations and can sit and dry such a bird as the Fairy Swallow then it is obvious that this is the type of pigeon that would suit you best. On the other hand if you are no good at this sort of thing and require a variety of bird that needs the minimum of getting ready, you would probably be better off with a flying breed such as the Roller or Tippler.

The fancier cannot alter the shape of a pigeon, merely aid good condition and add the finishing touches. Show preparation is definitely an art and it cannot be mastered overnight. It takes many years before fanciers can say that they can prepare a pigeon to their utmost satisfaction.

Washing

Washing pigeons in readiness for showing is not always advisable because it can destroy the oily content of the feathers, making them dry and brittle. Washing should therefore only be carried out as a last resort if the pigeon in question is very soiled.

Firstly, it is better to use warm water straight from the tap because cold water could cause the bird to catch a chill as it will be soaked thoroughly. The bird should be gently lowered into a washing-up bowl of warm water and, with one hand holding the pigeon, the other should pour water over the bird from a small cup or jug. When the bird is completely wet through it should have some soft soap rubbed over it such as baby soap or soap powder that is made for washing soft delicate fabrics. Anything that contains bleaches or anything caustic should never on any account ever be used.

Rub the soap all over the bird ensuring that the head and eyes of the pigeon are protected.

The region of the bird's body that is particularly soiled should be given attention. After the pigeon has been washed it should be rinsed thoroughly to make sure that all traces of soap have been removed, this is very important. If soap is left on the plumage it will harden as the bird dries and will make the feathers brittle and unsightly.

After rinsing the pigeon should be placed in a warm towel and dabbed and patted to remove the excess water from its feathers.

The pigeon is now placed into a basket or box that has had newspaper placed on the floor, and the basket is placed in front of a radiator or fire. Make sure that the basket or box is not too near the heat by testing with your hands, if the basket feels warm move it back until there is just the hint of warmth on the outside surface.

As soon as the bird begins to preen itself it is a sign that the basket can be dispensed with, and the pigeon should now be placed into a show pen where the air can circulate and complete the drying process. This can be aided with the use of a hair dryer. The dryer should be held at such a distance that the bird feels a very slight warm breeze. Never under any circumstances hold the dryer so close as to frighten the pigeon otherwise it will begin to flap about in the pen, with the result that it could damage its feathers or, worse, break a flight or tail feather.

Do not try to force the drying process. Only when you are sure that the bird is perfectly dry should it be removed and replaced into the loft.

After washing, the pigeon feathers will be brittle and dry but when the bird preens it will put back the missing oils which are so vital to good feather condition. When washing a bird always make sure that it has at least three days to put back the oil by preening, before the pigeon is entered in any show. The bird's bloom will tell you when it can be shown with safety.

When preparing pigeons for the show pen, never try to cheat by putting something back that might be missing, or take anything away that should not be there. This is faking and it is frowned upon in any type of livestock showing.

There are, however, subtle differences between this and enhancing the bird's appearance. To do this requires the simplest of equipment and just a few minutes of the fancier's time. It is time well spent and can often mean the difference between winning a class and being an also-ran.

The Wattle and Eye Cere

The pigeon's wattle is the white spongy substance on top of the beak in front of the eyes. Sometimes the bird's wattle will become greasy and dirty. Greasy wattle is associated with the feeding of big youngsters and it can be a nuisance. If the wattle and eye cere are sprinkled with powdered chalk it will make all the difference to the head of the bird. Make quite sure that no chalk enters the bird's eye as this will set up an irritation and make the eye water, which will prevent the bird from being shown at all. If powdered chalk is not available ordinary kitchen corn flour can be used instead.

The Feet

It is an absolute waste of time trying to show a pigeon if it has got dirty feet. Nothing looks worse, and yet it can so easily be avoided.

Firstly, the feet should be washed in either an aqueous solution of iodine or vinegar. Whichever is used, ensure that all traces of dirt are removed and that the registration ring is clean and that the numbers and letters can be read with ease. Dry the feet with a clean cloth and smear them both with petroleum jelly (Vaseline). About an hour or two after this treatment it will be seen that the bird's feet and legs will be bright pink and look much more attractive than when they were covered with dirt and muck. The finishing touch can be added by applying black lead pencil to the toe nails (if the toe nails are black in colour anyway).

The feet of feather-legged breeds must be given very careful treatment. When the bird is washed prior to showing, the feet and legs must also receive some attention. These are the parts of the bird's anatomy that are most likely to be soiled. Although some birds may attempt to preen their foot feathers, it is best to brush them lightly after drying so that they will spread properly and therefore show to their best advantage when the bird is placed in the show pen.

Do not be afraid to pay attention to the bird's feet when penning your exhibits on the day of the show. Always carry a piece of clean lint material for wiping the feet, and a little petroleum jelly in a jar. This will ensure that your exhibit will stay in the condition in which you penned it and therefore stand a better chance in competition.

When handling pigeons that have been prepared for the

show pen, use a silk headscarf or clean towel; try and avoid handling too much or the bloom will be removed from the bird's feathers.

Show Pen Training

Before the exhibition pigeon can be shown in open competition, it must have had some type of pen training. Wild pigeons that are continually flapping about will never be awarded anything, they are a nuisance and often upset the other birds in neighbouring pens. Good pen training, then, is a must and should begin when the bird comes straight from the nest. The youngsters can be placed in the training pen to accustom them to its confines.

At first this can be done in groups if there are a number of young birds of the same age together in the loft. The merits of each particular bird can be assessed whilst this is going on and the future show champion picked out. Leave these youngsters in the pen for an hour or so every day and whilst they are there, soothe them by talking to them and offering them a seed mixture that they particularly like.

After a day or two of this treatment the youngsters can be separated and each put into a pen of its own. At first they will try and get through the wires to each other but after a while they will realise that this is not possible and they will settle down. Again soothe them by talking and offering them some seed. It is vital that nothing upsets the youngsters at this stage because they will become pen-shy if they are frightened. It is a good plan to place the pens in a garden shed or garage where it is quiet and restful. Do make sure that the birds are not disturbed, particularly by a dog or cat.

When the young birds feel at home in the pen they are ready to spend a night in there, so it is a good idea to supply them with drinking vessels. Special water pots can be purchased that will hook onto the wire of the showpen making it impossible for the bird to spill any water and make a mess of its plumage. The bird's food can be scattered on the pen floor, but any that is not eaten straight away should be removed.

The general idea is to try and teach the bird that the show pen is merely an extension of everyday life, and that it need hold no fear for the bird. When the pigeons feel thoroughly accustomed to the pen, it is time to get them used to the judging stick. This device is used by all judges and is a telescopic metal rod that is used to prompt the pigeon to show to its best advantage. Use the judging stick very gently and stroke the bird with it whilst talking to it again. Push the stick under its tail and between its legs. Continue this treatment until the bird will accept the stick and begin to react to it whenever the stick is introduced.

All fancy pigeons have their own particular stance and they should be made to adopt this posture whenever they are touched with the judging stick. Any birds that do not adapt to this treatment will be failures on the show bench. Such birds, however, might make good stock birds and should be given every chance to prove their worth before being discarded.

Pigeon shows are not conducted in absolute silence and therefore some noise should not upset the birds too much. So it is a good idea that the birds should be subjected to some noise at home.

A portable radio placed near the show pens will give the birds something to get used to whilst they are in the training stages. The presence of people and other animals is also a matter which the best trained pigeons should be able to take in their stride. If other members of the family will agree, place the show pens in the house itself, in the kitchen perhaps, well away from food of course or in the lounge if at all possible. Anywhere that people gather will suit very well.

The training process might seem long-winded to the novice but will pay dividends later.

Never try and make do with second best when preparing your birds for the shows. If the fancier has done his part and made sure that the birds are in the pink of condition, then no blame can be attached to the fancier if failure should be the result. To be a good winner we firstly have to learn to be a good loser; it is much harder to lose than it is to win. As in all branches of livestock showing there are many setbacks and pitfalls; if they can be weathered and overcome the fancier is all the wiser for the experience.

The novice should try and learn what each particular judge considers of more importance and then exhibit birds under him which excel in this property. It is all a matter of horses for courses.

Never be afraid to ask questions of the more experienced fanciers; listen to what they have to say and follow their advice to the letter. This does not mean that the novice should not experiment. Such experiments are good for the novice and will show him in very real terms why this or that should be done, or why it should not be done.

7

Fancy and Flying Breeds

Exhibition pigeons are divided roughly into two groups, these being the normal exhibition type of birds, and the flying breeds.

The flying breeds are those that can be allowed their liberty and will in fact fly around the loft for exercise. In these types of pigeon the homing sense is developed more than it is in the purely exhibition breeds. The exhibition breeds, if allowed their liberty, would merely fly blindly until they were hopelessly lost. This type of bird is better allowed the use of an aviary into which it can go to sunbathe and take some fresh air.

In fact all varieties of pigeon once had the ability to fly and home to their loft but man has gradually bred the instinct out of these birds. It is remarkable to think that the carrier once was the homing pigeon of the day and in fact the modern racing pigeon is an ancestor of the old English Carrier Pigeon. The modern day carrier would be unable to see very well if it were allowed its liberty because of the size of its walnut-shaped wattle. Whether this bird would still possess some homing ability is very doubtful.

It is also a remarkable feature of some fancy pigeons, as they are better known, that they cannot feed their own young. This trait is peculiar to the Chinese Owls, the Satinettes and the Blondinettes. The face of these birds is very flat and the beak is the same shape as that of the budgerigar and parrot. These breeds have to have their young reared by foster parents which usually are crosses of other fancy breeds or racing pigeons that have been discarded.

Fig. 16   The English Carrier Pigeon

Flying Breeds

The Tippler

The Tippler is a small type of pigeon that resembles the racing pigeon with the exception that the Tippler is more slightly built, the eyes are more often orange, and the beak and wattle are finer.

The flying Tippler is famous for its ability to fly over the loft area for hours on end. This type of Tippler is in fact the competition bird which competes in competitions to see whose pigeons can fly the longest. The birds are formed into a kit of three individuals and they are released at first light early in the morning. The kit will fly overhead until they are given the signal to come down which is usually the appearance of a white bird on the loft roof or sometimes a flag is waved. Flights of fourteen hours duration are not uncommon. The usual colour of the competition Tippler is like that of the racing pigeon being blue, blue chequered, black and silver as well as the occasional grizzle and red.

The exhibition Flying Tippler is perhaps slightly larger than its compatriot the competition Tippler. The colour differs in that the show type usually appears in what is

Fig. 17 The 'Print' Flying Tippler

termed as a print. This is in fact a white pigeon that has grey coloured wing flights and tail, the neck is the usual greenish purple colour of all pigeons. The bird's body should be pure white and any foreign coloured feathers are usually taken out before the bird is put into the show pen. Self colours are also known in the show type flying Tippler. The more usual colour is black but yellows are seen now and again, but not as much as they used to be.

There is yet another type of Tippler and that is the true show Tippler which is even larger than the variety just described because special attention is paid to the general shape of the bird. The head for instance is much more exaggerated and rounded, as is the general outline of the bird's body. The more usual colour of the Show Tippler is mottled which is in fact a white bird that is mottled with feathers of a solid colour such as black or brown.

The Birmingham Roller

The Roller, as it is more often termed, was bred for its ability to perform somersaults whilst flying through the air. It is a very old breed and as its name implies it was bred around the Birmingham area of England. The tumbling ability of these birds has to be seen to be believed as they will fly to a great height before beginning to perform. The somersaults are executed one after the other until the bird loses height and has to begin to fly to prevent itself hitting the ground. This may sound a bit exaggerated but in fact many birds have been killed or injured through not pulling out of their spin fast enough and actually dashing themselves against the ground.

In appearance the Birmingham Roller is very much like the Tippler except that it is perhaps slimmer and slightly longer cast in feather. The exhibition type of Roller is bred in a wide variety of colours of which the most popular is the badge. Here the bird may be of any colour but the head and breast of the bird are white making a very interesting contrast on a dark coloured bird.

The Birmingham Roller is perhaps the most popular of the flying breeds that are regularly exhibited in England.

The Short Faced Tumbler

The Tumbler is a large pigeon with many different types and the most popular of the tumblers is the short faced.

This bird is in fact the original tumbler that was bred for its flying and tumbling abilities many years ago in England.

Fig. 18 The Muffed Tumbler. This is in fact a short-faced Tumbler which is 'muffed', i.e. feather-legged.

There is no record of where this bird was first flown, as there is with the Birmingham Roller, although it is near certain that it was developed at about the same time and probably within the same area. Most tumblers of today will fly but cannot tumble as often or as deep as they used to; they are more exhibition birds. The short faced variety is very much like the Roller in appearance although it is perhaps slightly smaller and more thickset in build.

The head and face of the short faced tumbler are thick set and much pronounced at the forehead. The short faced tumbler has a beak that is very similar to that of the Roller making it likely that their breeding was connected in the early days. The more usual colours of the short faced tumbler are also those of the Roller but as well as the badge there are also other distinguishing features or markings known as kite, agate, and bearded.

The Long Faced Tumbler

Yet another form of tumbler which is bred for its showing prowess rather than its flying ability, the long faced tumbler is even more thick set than its short faced counterpart. The head and face are particularly rounded, the beak much more shortened and thicker.

The long faced tumbler is usually bred in solid colours in red, black, yellow or almond. The head is half coloured and half white giving the bird the alternative name of Bald Tumbler.

The Parlour Tumbler

This type of tumbler is not very often seen today and may even be extinct. The background of the bird is rather obscure but it is certainly an English creation as the term parlour refers to the room of a house and in European countries the bird has been referred to as the House Tumbler. This bird is very typical of the types just described but it has the peculiarity of being able to jump up in the air from a standing position, somersault, and land back on its feet where it started from!

German Toys

These pigeons are not often seen in this country but they are in fact a form of tumbler with slight bodies, elongated faces and very short thickset beaks. Many of these tumblers are feather legged and have some kind of crest or head adornment.

Tumblers are popular pets right across all countries of the world and there are weird and wonderful varieties to be seen, particularly in the Middle East. In these countries the birds are kept in lofts on the house roof.

Exhibition Breeds

The Turbit

The Turbit is certainly a pigeon of European origins but exactly where it came from nobody knows for certain. The bird itself is about the size of a tumbler but has a frill of feathers which run along the nape of the neck and ends in a type of crest. There is also a frill on the breast but it is not nearly so pronounced as in other breeds. The usual colour of the Turbit is white with a coloured wing which is usually blue or black. There are other colours which are red, yellow or dun.

Because the Turbit is relatively short beaked it is a good idea to provide it with foster parents during the breeding season.

The Fairy Swallow

This is in fact a member of the Tumbler family and also a German toy variety. The bird is very long in feather and has long sweeping wings which are splayed over the back. Distinguishing marks include a cowl of feathers around the head and very long delicate foot feathers which can measure anything up to three inches in length (7 centimetres). The general colour of the Fairy Swallow is white with coloured wings, flights and feet feathers. The skull at the forehead is also coloured giving the bird a very unusual appearance.

Pouters and Croppers

These are a group of pigeons which have the ability to blow their crops up when in display. The family is large and there are many variations.

Fig. 19 The Pouter

English Pouters

This is the most popular of the Pouters, it is tall and erect when in display. The crop is large and rounded, the waist thin, and the legs are long and slender. The English Pouter also has a cluster of white feathers on the wing butts which are known as the rose pattern. Pouters are bred in blue, black, red, yellow and white.

Pigmy Pouter

This is in fact a smaller version of the English Pouter and even comes in the same colour range. Pouters in general are very friendly pigeons and can become very affectionate towards their owners. They do not however make good parents because they neglect their eggs and young in preference for strutting about the loft.

Dutch Cropper

This bird is sometimes referred to as the Old Holland Pouter because it originated in the Netherlands and is credited with being the forerunner of the English and Pygmy Pouters. The bird itself is long and lean looking and, when in display, stands tall and erect. The feet and legs are covered with ornate muffs which are long and sweeping and extend right up as far as the thighs. The Old Holland Cropper comes in a wide variety of colours intermingled with white.

Holle Cropper

This bird is not at all like the other Pouters or Croppers that have just been described. In fact it is small and rounded whereas the others are tall and elongated. The Holle Cropper holds its head erect when in display so that the globe is in actual fact the highest part of its body. The Holle Cropper is bred in solid colours such as red, yellow and white. It is also bred in patterned types such as blue-barred and chequered.

Oriental Frills

These are the birds that I described briefly elsewhere as

Fig. 20 The Oriental Frill

being unable to feed their own young. There is no doubt that the breeds originated in or around Turkey and that they were brought to this country many, many years ago by travellers and discoverers.

All these birds have a frill of feathers which runs down the breast of the bird and a crest of feathers which ends in a point above the head. They are nearly all grouse legged which means that they have feathers down their legs but they do not cover the feet.

The face of the bird is its most unusual feature in that it is completely rounded with just the smallest trace of a wattle and beak.

Satinettes

The markings of this bird are of a white background and multicoloured wings and wing butts, and tail.

The Blondinettes

The shape of the bird is similar to other Oriental Frills but the body is pale blue and not white as in the satinettes.

The Owl

This is not a bird of prey as might be expected but a very attractive fancy pigeon with the same facial characteristics as the Oriental Frills. There are three types of Owl, these being: Chinese, English and African Owls. It is not known exactly where these birds came from but there is a record of African Owls being imported into England from Tunis in 1858. Unlike the Oriental Frill the Owl is clean legged and does not

Fig. 21   The Nun

have the frill of feathers on the nape of the neck. There is however a breast frill and the wing coverts are laced at the edges of each feather. Being extremely short beaked the owl cannot feed its own young and therefore foster parents are required for successful breeding.

The Nun

The Nun is without doubt the most popular fancy pigeon of them all, it is very easy to breed and very friendly towards its keeper. In appearance the Nun is very similar to the Flying Tippler except that the Nun has a pearl coloured eye and a cowl of feathers at the back of the head. The head, face and breast of the Nun are coloured as are the flight feathers and tail feathers. The usual colours are red, yellow and black. Competition in Nun circles is very keen and they are bred to the highest standards. Those that win at the principal shows are very good specimens indeed and deserve every accolade.

Modena

This is an ancient flying breed which used to be flown in competition in the fourteenth century. It is named after the city of Modena in Italy from where it originated. The bird is very short and cobby in appearance with the plane of the back held perfectly horizontal. The Modena's tail is quite short and wide, the flight feathers of the wing meet at the edge of the tail. The neck is thick and shortened and the breast full and sweeping down to a full broad chest. When in stance the bird stands with its feet planted firmly apart and on tiptoe.

There are two main patterns in the Modena. One is the Gazzi, which is a white pigeon with a coloured head, wings and tail. The feathers of the wing butts are delicately laced along their edge and the flight feathers are smudged with black. The other colour of Modena is Schietti which is solid coloured throughout with no pattern of any kind.

It is interesting to note that there are no less than one hundred and fifty two colour varieties of the Modena.

Fig. 22   The Modena

The Lahore

The Lahore is a Far Eastern breed of pigeon which originates from the city of Shiraz which is actually in Iran. The name of Lahore was probably given to the bird because it was very popular with the pigeon keepers of that city many years ago.

In appearance it is very much like a giant tumbler with long cast wings and tail. The colour is solid with the exception of white underparts beginning on the face and reaching as far as the all white tail. The Lahore is becoming very popular in this country and comes in a wide variety of colours including an attractive Lavender.

Fantail

This is one of the most common pigeons; it can be found in gardens and parks and makes a fascinating and unusual pet.

Fig. 23 The Fantail

The Fantail originated from India where it is known as the shaker. It is in fact the ballet dancer of the pigeon world as it struts to and fro with its neck shaking and twitching and huge fan-shaped tail displayed like a miniature peacock. The Fantail has a full well-rounded chest and slender body giving it an almost unbalanced appearance. The small head is carried well back and in good specimens the head is buried by the breast as the bird displays. It is said that the Fantail has no oil gland at the base of the tail and this may indeed account for the papery feel of this pigeon's feathers.

The Fantail is bred in a wide variety of colours including a delicate powdered silver. During the breeding season the breeding stock have their tail feathers trimmed to allow for better fertility.

Dragoon

The Dragoon is a very old English breed of pigeon which was originally called the Horseman because of the wedge shaped head which is likened to a horse's head. The beak and face are held parallel to the ground. The Dragoon's wattle and eye cere are large and rugged giving the bird a look of the Carrier. The Dragoon type is short and thick-set with wide shoulders gradually tapering off to a square ended tail.

Besides the blues, chequers, grizzles and silvers, there are also red, yellow and white Dragoons. Young Dragoons have a fine textured wattle as do the hens. The adult cocks are magnificent birds and very proud in their stance and general outlook.

Dragoons are not difficult to breed from; their size and stature make them very hardy and robust.

The Carrier

This is perhaps one of the oldest breeds of pigeon in the world (illustrated Fig. 16, page 90). Although it is strictly an English variety of pigeon it is thought that the original birds came from somewhere in Iran in the Middle East. There is no mistaking the Carrier once it has become familiar to the fancier or the layman; it is a tall bird reaching a height of at least sixteen inches and probably more. The Carrier is slim built and yet gives the impression of a powerful bird. The feathers are tightly and closely grouped and the flesh hard to the touch. The most distinguishing feature of the Carrier is its huge wattle and eye cere. In a fully grown adult the wattle will resemble a large walnut both in shape, size and texture.

The eye cere too is massive and may reach a diameter of as much as an inch around the eye. The Carrier is truly a majestic and proud pigeon and was once referred to as the 'King of Pigeons'.

Many years ago this bird was used for carrying messages, hence its name which is a label that is nowadays attached to any kind of homing pigeon. The Carrier can be bred in red, white, yellow and Dun and makes a very interesting fancy pigeon for the novice.

The Antwerp

This is the bird from which the modern-day racing pigeon is evolved. It was first bred in Belgium but did not make its first appearance in England until around 1860. The Antwerp is a large bird, having amply proportioned shoulders and breast.

If the Antwerp were to be used as a racing bird today it would fit into the category of the sprinter as its flight feathers and tail are short yet very strong. The tail is carried clear of the ground by thick-set legs spread wide apart. The lines of the Antwerp are graceful and sweeping. The Antwerp Smerle has a frill of feathers down the breast giving it a very attractive appearance. The head is thick-set and strong and the beak short and blunt.

Other Varieties

There are many other varieties and breeds of fancy pigeon than those few mentioned here. It would be an impossible task to list and describe them all or even half of them. They have their own special charm and personalities which endear them to the people who breed them for the show pen. Likewise each has its own difficulties which are overcome in one way or another, for instance the difficulty of breeding from the very short faced varieties such as the Oriental Frills and the English and Chinese Owls. Whilst some birds can be flown out around the loft, others have to be kept in the confines of an aviary to allow them to gain the maximum benefit from the sun and fresh air. There are some varieties of fancy pigeon that have very rarely been seen in the U.K. or the United States of America, where there is a thriving Fancy Pigeon fellowship.

8

Ailments and Diseases

The modern-day pigeon fancier has the advantage of science with which to combat the diseases which afflict the pigeon.

Not so many years ago a pigeon fancier had to kill any of his stock that contracted a disease. In those days there had been very little research into the maladies which we now understand so well.

Perhaps the most famous of all pigeon diseases was the condition known as 'going light', which was in fact a method of describing the general decline of a sick bird. The pigeon that was going light went off its food and wasted away within a matter of days. Today we have come to realise that these symptoms are in fact attributable to a wide variety of conditions. Although each of these diseases have the same symptoms (going light) we can distinguish between them with the aid of observation and general good management.

Good animal husbandry will prevent the onset of disease no matter which type of livestock is kept. If the housing is in good order and the feeding and general welfare are correct, disease will find it difficult to gain a foothold.

Daily cleaning-out of the pigeon loft will keep the risk of disease to an absolute minimum but that does not mean to say that a disease cannot be contracted. Even the cleanest pigeon lofts have had their fair share of the misery that the common diseases can cause.

The fancier's ability to observe and note any oddities within his stock is the best safeguard of all. It is in fact an inborn ability of the successful fancier to note whenever a particular bird does not look its usual self, or if the droppings are not of the normal consistency and colour. If the suspect is confirmed as a disease carrier, then that bird must be kept well away from its fellows to prevent infection of the whole loft.

Cleanliness

The pigeon loft must be kept clean to have any chance of avoiding infection by disease; this is the basic requirement and the foundation of good management. If the pigeon loft is scraped out at least once per day then it can be classed as a clean loft. It is sometimes impossible for this to be carried out every day, and if so, provision must be made for feeding the birds in such a way that their food never comes into contact with any surface that has been soiled by the bird's own droppings. The easiest method of doing this is to provide the birds with food hoppers and ensure that the hopper is cleaned after use.

During warm weather it is more important than ever to ensure a high level of cleanliness. Flies will collect wherever there is the slightest chance of their finding something on which to feed. Pigeon droppings that are left on the floor all day will naturally attract flies, and these flies may have just visited somewhere where there is disease. The importance of removing the birds' droppings at the earliest possible chance becomes very obvious.

Disinfection

The pigeon fancier has at his disposal a very wide range of disinfectants and the range is very confusing. As well as the products advertised by the veterinary chemists there are also a fine range of household products which will serve him very well.

The idea of a disinfectant is to kill any germs that might be present within the loft. It is therefore wise policy to choose the product that has been prepared by the veterinary chemist because it will have been tried and tested on the very same organisms and germs that the fancier is likely to be faced with.

Total disinfection is almost impossible to achieve, but the fancier can go a long way towards this if the right application of the disinfectant is used. For instance it would be wrong to wipe all loft interior surfaces with a damp cloth that has been soaked with disinfectant. All that this would do is spread the germs even further.

Complete saturation of the loft interior should be the aim of total disinfection. There should be no hiding place for germs if you are to keep disease at bay. The only really effective method of disinfecting the interior of a pigeon loft is to spray it.

The modern hand-held spray is a boon and it is very simple to use with good results. The disinfectant is merely mixed with the correct amount of water and poured into the spray container. The head of the spray containing the trigger is then screwed into position and the gun is ready for use. The floor and perches of the loft should be sprayed whenever the opportunity arises and especially after scraping out. Once a month the whole interior of the loft should be sprayed including the walls and ceiling.

All feeding appliances and tools should be completely immersed in a bath of disinfectant at least once per week.

Observation

A sick pigeon will quickly go off its food and will sit huddled with all its feathers fluffed out as though it were cold. These are the classic symptoms that all is not well. As soon as this is seen to be happening the bird should be inspected for any obvious signs of disease or other cause of ill-health. Firstly, the eyes: they should be bright and clear with no sign of wateriness or discharge of any kind from them. The pigeon's wattle should be inspected, and it should be clean and white in colour. It should never be greasy unless the pigeon in question is feeding youngsters in the nest. The bird's beak should be clean and the inside of the throat clear of any obstruction. The throat should be a bright pink colour and the bird's breath should not be offensive.

The general condition of the bird's plumage should be noted; the feathers should be tight and be covered with a powdery substance known as bloom. Finally the bird's feet should be as clean as possible and also covered with powdery bloom. A pigeon that has bright red feet cannot be in good condition because its feet will be hot to the touch when they should be cold.

Preventing infection

Besides disinfection there are other measures that the fancier can take to help prevent the spread of disease within the pigeon loft.

Firstly, all fanciers must have provision for separating a pigeon that is suspect. Even if these measures are the use of a wooden box, provided that it is sited well away from the loft and its other inmates it will serve a very good purpose.

It would be of no benefit if a sick bird was allowed to stay within the same loft as other healthy birds even though direct contact is prevented. This measure will not prevent the spread of disease by airborne germs.

Another closely linked method of preventing infestation is to inspect thoroughly all new pigeons that are brought into the loft. Even though these pigeons may have come from lofts that are kept very clean, it can be that the new bird is a carrier of disease without showing any symptoms. It suffers from the disease but this cannot be detected visually. Again the bird must be kept apart from the rest of your stock until such time as you are convinced that the pigeon is disease free and healthy.

The racing pigeon fancier is constantly faced with the question of strays entering the loft. These birds, although they may be lost, tired and hungry pose the greatest threat of all. Racing pigeons that have spent some time in the open working their way back to their home lofts are easy prey for all kinds of sickness and disease. Certainly these birds will carry quite an amount of parasites in their plumage.

It is no good saying that these strays should never be allowed to enter the loft because they often come in with the other birds and are not noticed until perhaps later at feeding time.

Such strays should be caught up straight away and placed in a box that is kept for the purpose. The bird can then be fed and watered and set free the next morning to give it every chance to make its way back home. Feral pigeons are a different kettle of fish and should never be allowed anywhere near the loft and birds.

Diseases

Only the most common diseases are described here as it would take a volume to describe all the known diseases that can affect the pigeon.

First, the diseases that are caused by bacteria, followed by those that are caused by parasites.

Pigeon Pox

Pigeon Pox is a disease that can be compared to fowl pox which is a disease that infects poultry.

The first symptoms of pigeon pox are the discovery of wart-like lesions or nodules around the eyes and wattles of an infected pigeon. Following this the diseased bird will begin to form cheese-like growths inside the mouth. These growths are very similar to those which appear as a result of canker of the throat (see page 112). The pigeon pox growths can be easily distinguished by the fact that they do not infect the throat, only the mouth of the bird. It has been known for pigeons to develop the spots around the eyes without the mouth infection and they have lived. Cases such as this are not rare and the bird will usually develop an immunity to pigeon pox. However when infection is widespread there is usually a case for destroying the whole stock as such infestations prove fatal in the end.

Pigeon pox is carried by mosquitos and gnats and usually flares up in very warm weather. The insects will bite at any exposed part of the pigeon and are especially attracted to sores and wounds. Tender parts of the facial skin that have been pecked by other birds will also prove attractive to the mosquito.

The disease should be treated by separating any suspect

birds and applying silver protein to the lesions of the head and mouth. Silver protein can be purchased from a dispensing chemist.

The virus can be spread on hands and clothes and therefore it is very important to wash thoroughly after holding sick pigeons.

It is an advantage to be able to wear an overall of some kind when treating pigeons that are affected by pigeon pox. It goes without saying that all tools and utensils within the loft should be thoroughly disinfected and kept in a clean state.

The disease can be prevented to a very great extent by having the stock vaccinated against the disease. The vaccine is quite new and can be bought through the local veterinary surgeon.

One Eye Cold

This malady is peculiar to the pigeon and is not known to infect other forms of poultry. It is not an infection of the eye as such but more of an inflammation of the cere around the eye. The skin around the eye will become greatly inflamed and cause the unfortunate pigeon to try and scratch at it. There are usually no other symptoms although occasionally a pigeon will be seen to sneeze. There are patent medications for this disease that can be bought from the vet. These are usually in tablet form and the infected bird will normally make a rapid recovery. One eye cold is very infectious and it is wise policy to separate any suspect birds straight away rather than waiting to confirm the disease.

Ornithosis

This is a disease that is caused by a virus rather than bacteria. It is commonly associated with budgerigars and parrots and when it attacks these birds it is called psittacosis. There have been cases when it has infected the fancier himself and it has had the same symptoms as influenza.

The symptoms are the appearance of a discharge from one or both eyes of the infected bird with a result that the eyes become inflamed. If neglected the disease will blind the pigeon and diarrhoea will ensue causing the bird a long lingering death unless it is disposed of quickly and painlessly. There is no definite method of confirming the disease unless microscopic tests are undertaken. Ornithosis can be successfully treated with an antibiotic known as 'oxytetracycline' by your vet.

Paratyphoid

This disease is more commonly known as salmonellosis and is bacterial. It is often a disease of young pigeons and is capable of killing them before the fancier has any idea that there is anything the matter with the stock. They die before showing any symptoms. Often older birds contract the disease with the result that they develop sores or abscesses on parts of the body. The sores are more common on the wing joints but they have been known to grow on the head giving the bird bouts of vertigo when it cannot stand unaided. Pigeons which show any of these symptoms should be discarded and certainly never bred from. There are antibiotics that can be used in the treatment of this disease but they have to be obtained from the vet.

Internal Parasites

Canker

The canker which infects pigeons has symptoms very like those of pigeon pox. There are in fact three distinct forms of canker, these being pharyngeal which infects the throat, the internal form which infects the liver amongst other organs, and the navel form which is seen in young pigeons, especially squeakers that are still in the nest.

The disease is caused by a minute parasite which infects the digestive tract of the bird beginning in the throat. Very often the infected bird will form cheesy growths in the mouth and throat which give off an offensive smell. The microscopic parasite cannot live for very long outside the pigeon's body and so there is very little likelihood of the disease being passed through re-infection from one bird to another. The most likely form of infection is through the parent bird feeding its young.

There is now available on the market a medication in the form of capsules that are given to each bird individually. Young pigeons can be treated in the same manner although they will require less dosage.

Coccidiosis

Perhaps the most well known of all the pigeon diseases. At one time this disease was a certain killer and any bird that contracted it was doomed.

Recently, however, this disease has developed into more of a chronic affliction with the result that the pigeon does not show any visible symptoms but merely goes off form. The racing pigeon will home late week after week never showing its true capabilities.

The symptoms of the disease in its virulent form are a general going off colour. The pigeon's eye will become very pale and glazed, the flesh around the beak will take on an insipid appearance. The pigeon's plumage will lack any kind of lustre and appear drab.

The bird itself will lose condition, go off its food and appear dull and lifeless. The disease is caused by a minute parasite which destroys the lining of the bird's intestine allowing other bacteria to gain a foothold. The eggs of the coccidia are passed out of the pigeon amongst the bird's droppings and can live either on the loft floor or in the ground for some considerable time. Damp patches within the loft are a haven for these eggs and they will thrive under such agreeable conditions. Certainly other birds pick them up and re-infest the whole colony within a matter of days.

The eggs cannot be destroyed with ordinary disinfectants but will perish after the whole area has been treated with an iodophor based germicide. This, incidentally is the same sort of defence used against outbreaks of foot and mouth disease on many farms. There are tablets which are placed into the pigeon's drinking water which will quickly kill off any coccidia that are present within the pigeons' intestines. Both treatments must be carried out at the same time.

Roundworms

These internal parasites will be found in most pigeons at some time or other, but the danger lies in a gradual build-up caused through neglecting the vital task of routine worming. Worming of one's stock should be carried out as a regular routine at certain times throughout the year. One of the most important times when pigeons should be wormed is just before pairing up.

Certainly a general loss of form can be attributed to the presence of worms within the bird's body. Worms may never actually be seen in the birds' droppings but they can still be present. The worm *eggs* are indeed passed out of the body in the birds' droppings. The eggs do not become infective immediately but will lie for about one week before they become active. Pigeons that pick up such eggs during foraging are in fact helping to hatch out the worm because the eggs will hatch within the bird's body and develop into a worm within a matter of three weeks. The cycle is then repeated.

Symptoms of worm infestation are a general lack of interest in the pigeon's surroundings; it will sit huddled and be disinclined to fly. In very severe cases the worms will actually be dispelled with the droppings. Piperzine citrate is the best treatment for roundworm, and it can be put into the birds' drinking water and so the whole flock can be dosed at one time.

Hairworms

These parasites do much more damage than the round-worm as they live in the duodenum as well as the intestine. The hairworm as its name implies is very much like an ordinary hair. It is so slender that it is invisible to the naked eye. In length it will measure about one inch. It has been claimed that more concentrated doses of piperazine will clear hairworm, but the drug methyridine will certainly kill them off. Worming agents contained in today's modern medicines contain both the drugs mentioned and therefore both types of worm can be cleared at the same time.

Tapeworms

The tapeworm is about five to seven centimetres long and flattish in shape. This worm will attach itself to the lining of the intestine with the aid of hooks which protrude from its head. In severe cases the worm may be seen hanging from the pigeon's vent but in more usual circumstances segments of the worm are found in the infected birds' droppings.

This tapeworm's intermediate host is slugs or snails and therefore the loft area should be kept free of these pests. Treatment can be effected by using dichlorophen, and each individual bird must be dosed.

Feather Parasites

Mites

Mites can only be seen with the aid of a microscope; the only exception to this is the red mite. There are a number of mites which will infest pigeons in the U.K. The first of these is the depluming mite which attacks the feathers of the pigeon. After some time the feathers begin to rot and the condition then becomes known as feather rot. All parts of the pigeon are affected and the feathers literally fall from the unfortunate bird. There is now a feather rot cream on the market which is very effective against this parasite.

The quill mite will make its home in the quill of the feather at the base near the bird's skin. The mite will destroy the feather via the quill which will split causing the feather to fall out.

The scaly leg mite does not often attack the pigeon but it attacks fowl regularly. This mite will burrow into the bird's leg and makes its home under the scales of the legs and feet. The end result is that the scales are lifted and lumps and bumps ensue. Scaly leg cream can be readily bought over the counter at almost any good pet shop.

Red mites are the most horrible of all the parasites. The mite itself is grey in colour and lives in the walls of the loft during daylight hours. At night it will emerge and attack anything that is warm blooded. The mites will bite the skin and gorge themselves on the victims' blood causing the mite to change colour from grey to red. The only defence against these insects is the regular treatment of the birds and the loft with an insecticide that contains malathion.

Lice

Lice are common on pigeons, and they are large enough to be seen with the naked eye. If the wing of an infected pigeon is open the lice will be seen quite easily as dark shapes within the vanes of the bird's wing feathers. The lice feed off feather dust and flaked scales of skin.

Although lice are a nuisance their presence need not cause the novice fancier any alarm. There are times, however, when infestations can get out of hand and then it is more difficult to rid the birds of these pests. Racing pigeons should be checked whenever they return from a race as the lice are transferred from one bird to another whilst they are in the race pannier. As a matter of routine the whole stock should be dusted monthly with a powder made especially for the purpose which can be purchased from any pet shop, whether the birds show signs of lice or not.

First Aid

There will be times when it is useful to have an elementary knowledge of first aid. Perhaps the most common injury to pigeons are cuts and lacerations caused by telephone wires and cables, aerials and masts. The bird will usually be very severely bruised in the process but this is better left alone. Cuts and gashes can be swabbed with a general antiseptic and left to heal by themselves. If the fancier feels competent enough he or she may wish to undertake the stitching of a particularly nasty cut. A bowed needle will be required and some sutures made from fine fishing line. If this is done make sure that each stitch is inserted one at a time and also that they are not pulled too tight as this will cause the bird much discomfort. After stitching the bird should be isolated from its fellows and the wound left to heal. The stitches can be cut away when it is felt that healing is well under way and it will be safe to do so.

Fractures

Fractures of the leg can be splinted with small pieces of wood which are wound round with plaster impregnated bandage. The limb will set within a matter of a few weeks. Wings should be held to the body with an old sock that has had the toe cut off. The bird is placed in the sock and if need be it can be hung up somewhere so that it will not be bothered by other birds in the loft. Although broken wings usually mean the end of a showing or racing career the stricken bird will be able to fly again although it may be with some difficulty. Cases that are beyond the scope of the fancier should always be reported to your local veterinary surgeon.

Appendix

Publications

There are various publications that can be bought over the newsagent's counter. In the racing pigeon fancy there is the 'Racing Pigeon', which is in fact a weekly newspaper which covers all aspects of racing pigeons including topical articles and a month by month guide for the novice to regional news, and the results of all the local club races and of course the national races which are open to the whole of the country. The Racing Pigeon can be obtained from: The Editor, Colin Osman, 19 Doughty Street, London WC1N, 2PT.

There is also the 'British Homing World' which is the official journal of the 'Royal Pigeon Racing Association'. This too is a weekly newspaper type of publication which contains articles of interest written by leading fanciers, news and results from all over the United Kingdom. Both these papers have a section for advertisements where racing pigeons and all equipment can be bought and sold.

There are also letters pages where the ordinary fancier is invited to write in and air his own particular views on any subject pertaining to racing pigeons. The British Homing World can be obtained by writing to: The Editor, Ernest Harbourne, 26 High Street, Welshpool, Powys, SY21 7JP. In addition to these weekly papers there are also two monthly racing pigeon magazines entitled 'Racing Pigeon Pictorial' and 'Pigeon Racing Gazette'. The Pictorial can be obtained by writing to the editor of the 'Racing Pigeon' who also publish the 'Pictorial'. The Pigeon Racing Gazette can be obtained by writing to: The All British Pigeon Racing Publishing Co Ltd., St Georges Hall, 198 Brooklands Road, Weybridge, Surrey.

The Fancy Pigeon has its own publication in the form of 'Pigeons and Pigeon World' which is devoted to fancy and flying breeds of pigeon such as Rollers and Tipplers, etc. There are notes about various breed club activities and the results of the shows plus advice and articles for the novice fancier. Pigeons and Pigeon World can be obtained by writing to: Fancy Press Ltd, 32 Windsor Road, Godmanchester, Cambridgeshire, PE18, 8DD.

Racing Rings

These are supplied to the clubs by the Royal Pigeon Racing Association, and thence to club members.

INDEX

Other Paperfront titles about animals:

How To Have A Well-Mannered Dog
Choose/Bring Up Your Puppy
Right Way To Keep Dogs
Right Way To Keep Cats
Right Way To Keep Hamsters
Right Way To Keep Pet Fish
Right Way To Keep Pet Birds
Right Way To Keep Rabbits
Right Way To Ride a Horse
Practical Horsemanship In Show and Field
Right Way To Keep Ponies
Horsekeepers Encyclopedia
All uniform with this book

ELLIOT RIGHT WAY BOOKS, KINGSWOOD, SURREY, U.K.

ELLIOT RIGHT WAY BOOKS, KINGSWOOD, SURREY, U.K.

OUR PUBLISHING POLICY

HOW WE CHOOSE

Our policy is to consider every deserving manuscript and we can give special editorial help where an author is an authority on his subject but an inexperienced writer. We are rigorously selective in the choice of books we publish. We set the highest standards of editorial quality and accuracy. This means that a *Paperfront* is easy to understand and delightful to read. Where illustrations are necessary to convey points of detail, these are drawn up by a subject specialist artist from our panel.

HOW WE KEEP PRICES LOW

We aim for the big seller. This enables us to order enormous print runs and achieve the lowest price for you. Unfortunately, this means that you will not find in the *Paperfront* list any titles on obscure subjects of minority interest only. These could not be printed in large enough quantities to be sold for the low price at which we offer this series.

We sell almost all our *Paperfronts* at the same unit price. This saves a lot of fiddling about in our clerical departments and helps us to give you world-beating value. Under this system, the longer titles are offered at a price which we believe to be unmatched by any publisher in the world.

OUR DISTRIBUTION SYSTEM

Because of the competitive price, and the rapid turnover, *Paperfronts* are possibly the most profitable line a bookseller can handle. They are stocked by the best bookshops all over the world. It may be that your bookseller has run out of stock of a particular title. If so, he can order more from us at any time—we have a fine reputation for "same day" despatch, and we supply any order, however small (even a single copy), to any bookseller who has an account with us. We prefer you to buy from your bookseller, as this reminds him of the strong underlying public demand for *Paperfronts*. Members of the public who live in remote places, or who are housebound, or whose local bookseller is unco-operative, can order direct from us by post.

FREE

If you would like an up-to-date list of all paperfront titles currently available, send a stamped self-addressed envelope to
ELLIOT RIGHT WAY BOOKS, BRIGHTON RD.,
LOWER KINGSWOOD, SURREY, U.K.